SAVING JUSTICE

James Comey served as director of the FBI from 2013 to 2017, appointed to the post by President Barack Obama. He previously served as U.S. attorney for the Southern District of New York and the U.S. deputy attorney general in the administration of President George W. Bush. He lives in Virginia with his wife and family.

Also by James Comey

A Higher Loyalty

SAVING JUSTICE

TRUTH, TRANSPARENCY, AND TRUST

JAMES COMEY

PAN BOOKS

First published 2021 by Flatiron Books, New York

First published in the UK 2021 by Macmillan

This paperback edition first published 2022 by Pan Books
an imprint of Pan Macmillan
The Smithson, 6 Briset Street, London EC1M 5NR
EU representative: Macmillan Publishers Ireland Ltd, 1st Floor,
The Liffey Trust Centre, 117–126 Sheriff Street Upper,
Dublin 1, D01 YC43
Associated companies throughout the world
www.panmacmillan.com

ISBN 978-1-5290-6283-0

1 3 5 7 9 8 6 4 2

A CIP catalogue record for this book is available from the British Library.

Printed and bound by CPI Group (UK) Ltd, Croydon, CR0 4YY

Visit **www.panmacmillan.com** to read more about all our books
and to buy them. You will also find features, author interviews and
news of any author events, and you can sign up for e-newsletters
so that you're always first to hear about our new releases.

To my children and all the other young people who have dedicated
themselves to making the world a better place

CONTENTS

SAVING JUSTICE

INTRODUCTION

*The United States Attorney is the representative not of
an ordinary party to a controversy, but of a sovereignty whose
obligation to govern impartially is as compelling as its
obligation to govern at all.*

UNITED STATES SUPREME COURT, 1935

"PUTIN TOLD ME, 'We have some of the most beautiful hook-
ers in the world.'" Donald Trump sat there bracketed by Bill Clinton's gold Oval Office curtains, backlit by the fading late-afternoon
February light. After only seventeen days in office, he hadn't finished
decorating, but he liked gold and hated Obama, so his staff must have
figured the old Clinton curtains would do for now. I could see them
on either side of his bright, golden head, as he told me about Vladimir Putin's view of Russia's prostitutes.

I was director of the FBI, in the fourth year of a ten-year term.
My mission was to protect the country from its adversaries, including an aggressive Russia, which had worked to elect the man now
sitting across the *Resolute* desk from me, the one reminiscing to
the FBI's leader about an off-color conversation with the Russian
authoritarian.

Two weeks earlier, and just steps away, Donald Trump's national security adviser had blatantly lied to FBI agents about his conversations with the Russians. The Department of Justice was leaderless after Trump fired my boss, Acting Attorney General Sally Yates, for refusing to enforce his "Muslim ban" immigration order, which was still causing chaos at the nation's airports. The new president had already begun attacking the intelligence community, of which the FBI was a part. It wouldn't be long before he came for the entire Justice Department, which was trying to understand why all the lying, why all the links between people around Trump and Russia. The attacks on Justice and its values had just begun. It would go on for years, doing grievous damage to an indispensable American institution.

From the beginning, America built and nurtured institutions to find truth. For centuries, Lady Justice has been depicted wearing a blindfold. She seeks only to weigh the facts, and find the truth, without regard to the people before her. The Constitution gave federal judges jobs for life to protect them from any political pressure to lift the blindfold. The Department of Justice was built around the notion that federal prosecutors are, as the Supreme Court has explained, representing an idea—justice—not an ordinary client. And the attorney general is not the president's personal lawyer. In the words of Robert Jackson, a former Supreme Court justice who held the top Justice job and served as chief Nuremberg war crimes prosecutor after World War II, the attorney general "has a responsibility to others than the President. He is the legal officer of the United States."

Like America, the Department of Justice and the justice system more broadly have long been imperfect in pursuing inspiring ideals. People and the institutions they create always fall short, infected by biases, fears, and misguided passions. Justice has been no exception. Innocent people get convicted, too many brown and Black people go to jail, too many poor people lack decent representation in a system where the quality of justice often varies with the quality of your lawyer. There is a lot wrong with justice in America. But one of the things that has been right with American justice is the reality and reputation built by the United States Department of Justice over generations. Across those decades, and especially in the nearly five decades since Watergate, Justice employees came to be seen as a people apart—still flawed in all the ways humans are flawed, but somehow different and trustworthy. They could be trusted to sort out the most difficult situations, to investigate politicians, to wade into painful racial strife, to find and tell the American people the truth.

If Justice Department employees are no longer seen as something separate in American life, we are all less safe. If jurors, judges, victims, witnesses, communities, and cops come to see them as part of a political tribe, and so trust them less, something essential is lost.

Donald Trump, aided by his attorney general, William P. Barr, severely undermined the nation's trust in the Department of Justice. Trump wasn't good at much, but he had an extraordinary ability to relentlessly cut at people and institutions he saw as threats. His death-by-a-thousand-lies approach was initially frustrated by his first attorney general, Jeff Sessions, who, for all his flaws, held to long-standing norms. He wouldn't order prosecutions the president wanted, and he stepped aside from the investigation of Russian interference because he had been a key member of the Trump campaign. When Trump fired Sessions, his replacement, Bill Barr, showed no such sensitivity to the department's values. From the beginning, Barr echoed the president, aping his dishonest characterizations of the department's work and appearing to respond to President Trump's self-interested demands for investigations and prosecutions. The Department of Justice was damaged by that. It was damaged again when the attorney general misled the American people about the work of the special counsel investigating the president. And again when the attorney general intervened in a case involving one of the president's friends to overrule the sentencing recommendation of career prosecutors. And again when the attorney general intervened in an effort to drop a case in which a political ally of the president had already pleaded guilty, twice.

If we are to be a healthy nation, the damage must be repaired. This book is an attempt to help with that vital task—to remind Americans of how the institutions of justice should work, and how their leaders should behave. I've had the good fortune to work in government in Republican and Democratic administrations—as a junior federal prosecutor, a United States Attorney, a Justice Department official, and the director of the FBI—and will share stories from my work that illuminate the vital core values of American justice and why we must overcome and repair the corrosive damage Trump and his underlings have done with dishonesty, cronyism, political payback, and amorality.

I started my career in the Department of Justice as a federal prosecutor in Manhattan, where I handled many cases over six years and learned searing lessons—from my supervisors, my colleagues, and my own mistakes—about the Justice Department's obligation to tell the whole truth at all times, to force witnesses to do the same, and to care more about doing justice than winning. Next, three years as a private lawyer at a law firm taught me how hard defense work is, and reminded me that government prosecutors don't have a client in the normal sense of that word; instead, they represent the idea of justice. When I then returned to the Department of Justice as a federal prosecutor in Virginia for six more years, I still prosecuted cases—and learned that part of telling the truth is keeping promises—but my work was increasingly about leading others in the department, about the bigger picture of our impact on communities. I came to see that public trust in the Department of Justice was everything; without it, we couldn't do the essential work of keeping people safe. And to foster that trust, it wasn't enough just to tell the truth in courtrooms. We were obligated to be transparent, to tell our fellow citizens what we were doing, and why.

When I became the chief federal prosecutor in Manhattan after 9/11, and then the number-two person—the deputy attorney general—at the Department of Justice in Washington, I learned that a vital part of maintaining public trust was ensuring that politics played no role in our decisions. Although the department was led by political appointees—something I was, for the first time, in both New York and Washington—our work had to be apolitical. To be effective, we needed to be seen as separate and apart from political tribes, making decisions based only on the facts and the law. And to assure the American people of that, we had to show them our work.

When I became FBI director in a deeply polarized America, the need to show our work and tell the truth—including about heartbreaking mistakes—was more important to the country's trust than ever. If there was to be justice in America, we could not be on anyone's team, or personally loyal to any leader, including the president.

The stories in this book are about success and failure, facts and falsehoods, constraint and oversight. These stories cover painful lessons that the whole truth must be at the center of our justice system, and about gut-wrenching errors by a very human institution. They are about discovering that a different set of obligations comes with representing the American people, who are no ordinary clients. They are stories to illustrate that political appointees can be faithful stewards of an apolitical Justice Department, and the costs when they fail to meet that obligation. And, most of all, they are stories to show that truth is real and it must be sought and spoken—in courtrooms, conference rooms, and investigative interviews—without regard to privilege, connection, or partisan allegiance.

Restoring the primacy of truth in those places, and rebuilding trust in the post-Trump era, is what this book is about. After January 20, 2021, Donald Trump will no longer be president. The institutions of justice he attempted to degrade—the concept of truth he attacked—must be repaired and strengthened. Like a virus, the pandemic of lies will return—too many slippery people have gained power and money from it, so they will attempt to use it again. To be ready, our institutions must be stronger and more resilient. This book—which is written for ordinary citizens, not legal experts or historians, because all of us must know the Justice Department—is about why we must do that, and how.

PART ONE

Learning Justice

As a junior federal prosecutor in Manhattan, I discovered core values of the Department of Justice: always tell the truth, all of it; insist that witnesses do the same, no matter how much they resist; never make an argument or take a case you don't believe in; and treasure constraint and oversight of your power. But it really all boils down to one thing: remember who your client is. I had to learn that I wasn't representing an investigator, a witness, my bosses, or even myself. I was representing something bigger and more important—justice. The American people expected me to care more about achieving the right result than winning.

CHAPTER I

THE GOOD DAYS

*God, grant me the serenity to accept the things I cannot change,
the courage to change the things I can, and the wisdom
to know the difference.*
REINHOLD NIEBUHR

THE MAN ON THE MOPED JUST grabbed her and drove away. Her little sister ran screaming into the house to tell their mother, who ran into the driveway, where the girls had been playing. But the street was quiet; her beautiful six-year-old daughter, the one with the shoulder-length brown hair and enormous eyes, was gone.

Kidnapping by a stranger is rare, but on the afternoon of Wednesday, September 14, 2016, it happened at the end of a suburban driveway in Wilmington, North Carolina. A convicted sex offender, who lived nearby after serving sixteen years in prison in North Carolina for molesting another six-year-old, had grabbed the little girl. He headed for a patch of thick woods, passing a school bus just before he turned off the paved road and drove deep into the trees. But we didn't know any of that yet.

Stranger kidnapping is also deadly. Law enforcement knows that if the child isn't found quickly, she will likely never be found alive. A frantic search began, with the local FBI office joining in to assist the county sheriff. News stations broadcast the Amber Alert. Volunteers and officers searched in a heavy rain through the night.

At FBI headquarters the next morning, during my regular senior staff meeting, Steve Richardson, the assistant director in charge of the Criminal Investigation Division, told me about the little girl who had been kidnapped in North Carolina sixteen hours earlier. He explained that our Wilmington staff had worked through the night, doing what we could to help our local partners, but there was no sign of the little girl. We had a suspect—a convicted child molester who owned a moped—but this was likely to end very badly. I said, "What a world," and asked him to keep me informed.

Two hours later, Richardson walked quickly into my office. "They found her," he said, laying an eight-by-ten color photograph in front of me. "And she's alive." I looked down at the large picture. The little girl looked directly at me. Her strikingly large eyes were wide open; her face, still beautiful even covered in mosquito bites, was impassive, like she didn't know what was happening. She was looking up at the officer who recorded the scene as other officers used an electric saw to cut the thick chain around her neck cinching her to the tree I could see just inches away from her head. Her torso was covered with an officer's rain jacket, put there to cover her skin, which was raw from a night of exposure to water and insects.

I started crying. I couldn't look away from the picture. I held my hand up, palm to Richardson, to thank him and ask him to leave, all without words. He said, "Boss, these are the good days," and left. I kept staring at the picture. I thought of the girl and her sister and her parents and my own children and all the children who are not found and not saved.

She was saved by a tip. After the night of searching in a downpour, investigators heard from a school bus driver, who recalled seeing a man and a little girl on a moped near a wooded area the previous afternoon. Two sheriff's deputies responded to the spot. Sergeant Sean Dixon brought his Hanoverian tracking hound, Bane. He let Bane smell the little girl's Catholic school uniform and pillowcase before they plunged into the trees. Two hundred yards into the woods, Lieutenant J. S. Croom, working without a dog, saw her first, curled into the fetal position, her arms and legs pulled into her pink shirt, a thick chain binding her neck to a sugar oak tree. Certain she was dead, he called out to Dixon and ran toward the body. "Just the tone of his voice and the way he called my name, I knew he found something," Dixon said. "My heart kinda dropped." Croom later testified that he touched the still form on the ground. "And she snapped her head around and her eyes were ginormous and she said, 'Are you here to help me and take me to my mama?'" Through the trees, Dixon heard Croom again, shouting that the child was alive, she was alive.

"She was the strongest little girl I'd ever seen in my life," Dixon testified. "She just stared at me. I asked her if she was cold, and she said yes. She was soaking wet. She had mosquito bites all over her body." Officers stopped a passing contractor truck and borrowed a battery-operated Sawzall. Dixon put his fingers between the tree and the chain and Croom sawed through it. The child was rushed to the hospital. Croom stood by the sugar oak and cried. Now I was in my office, staring at the little girl and crying.

Forty-seven-year-old Douglas Nelson Edwards was convicted and sentenced to prison for kidnapping, attempted murder, and sexual assault of a child. He will not hurt another child. This was one of the good days. This was why we did this work.

I never planned to be part of the Department of Justice. I knew only that I wanted to get a law degree and help people. But I didn't know how I might do that. My first job out of law school showed me. I became a judicial clerk—a fancy way of saying "judge's assistant"—for a federal trial judge in the Southern District of New York, which includes Manhattan and other big pieces of the city and its northern suburbs. My job was to spend a year helping the judge with legal research and writing.

Clerkships are prestigious jobs for young lawyers, usually reserved for academic stars. I had done fine in law school, but I wasn't a star, which explained why dozens of judges rejected my applications. The judge who hired me, John M. Walker Jr., was brand-new, appointed during my last year of law school. He had been serving as assistant secretary of the treasury when Ronald Reagan—whose vice president, George Herbert Walker Bush, was the judge's first cousin—appointed him to be a federal judge. The timing worked well for me, because Judge Walker was looking for his very first law clerks at a time when the academic stars already had clerkships lined up. To be honest, he was slightly desperate, and so was I. Thereafter, for the next several decades, he hired people with stronger academic records.

As a new federal judge, Walker was eager to do well. And, despite his own impressive credentials, he came into office with a whiff of nepotism in the air, which he worked to dispel. The judge spent twelve hours each workday in the courthouse, and usually came in at least one weekend day. My co-clerk and I were expected to be there whenever he was, which was constantly. I was twenty-five and it was wearing me out. We thought he should—and we should—get out more. The judge was a forty-five-year-old single guy in the big city— handsome, with money and a job the United States Constitution said was his for life. What was not to like? He left his suit jacket hanging in his office when he donned his robe to take the courtroom bench. I would slip into his office on the pretense of dropping off a draft memo about a case and slide his leather-bound pocket calendar from his jacket pocket to see if he had a date that evening. If he did, we could.

During the summer of our clerkship year, he was gone for an entire workday at some judicial training. My co-clerk and I were at our desks, which faced each other in a small room. I looked up from some thick book with microscopic writing.

"Let's go to the beach."

Jack chuckled.

"I'm serious, let's go. We'll grab some stuff at my apartment and take my car." My place in Hoboken, New Jersey, was on the way to the beach town of Spring Lake, where we had a fractional share of a summer beach house rental with a dozen friends. We knew the judge's calendar; he wouldn't be in today. "When are we ever going to get the chance again?"

"Yeah, grab *your* stuff. I got no stuff." He was right; his apartment was far in the wrong direction, up by Columbia University. I could loan him shorts and a shirt, but my shoes were far too big.

"Wait a minute. I have an idea." Jack and the judge were the same size. I returned from the judge's private office holding his running shoes, which he sometimes used to exercise before court. "We both got stuff. Let's go."

It was an incredible weekday at the Jersey shore. A Ferris Bueller day off. We swam, shot baskets, ran on the beach. And never got caught. Very, very early the next morning, I put the judge's sneakers back in his closet.

In hindsight, I should have slapped the soles of the judge's shoes together a time or two, out on the street. For decades, Judge Walker wondered why, on a warm Manhattan morning, wearing Nikes that had never been out of the city, his shoes left a ghostly track of sand silhouettes across the dark blue carpet of his judicial office.

He mentioned it to his secretary, who shrugged, but we were very lucky that he never thought to ask us.

At the start of his legal career, Judge Walker had been an Assistant United States Attorney for the Southern District of New York. He told stories from those days, with a mix of joy and sorrow. It had been the best job he ever had. The work, the friendships, the case stories. There was nothing like it. He would get almost misty-eyed speaking about the role and "the Office," with reverence.

I could see what he meant when we sat in the courtroom to watch cases be argued. We saw a lot of bad lawyers—many were sloppy, unprepared, late, slippery, even disrespectful. There was something different about the women and men from the U.S. Attorney's Office. They were almost always younger than the other lawyers and stood straighter, buttoned their jackets more quickly, answered more directly, met deadlines, and admitted what they didn't know. If they were corrected or admonished, they answered, "Yes, Your Honor," and didn't do it again.

But there was more to it than style points. I noticed that the judge—and even opposing lawyers—believed what these federal prosecutors said. If they described the facts or legal conclusions of a particular court precedent, or explained what happened during a phone call, everyone in the courtroom accepted their recollection, even people who didn't know them. Something unseen vouched for them. It was strange, and, at twenty-five, I couldn't explain it. But I was drawn to that work. I wanted that life. At twenty-six, I got the chance, and lived it in different roles for the Department of Justice over much of the next thirty years, until I was fired as FBI director by Donald Trump.

———

I loved working at the Department of Justice, and the FBI, which is only one of the components of the department. The organization is extraordinarily complex, made up of more than one hundred thousand people all over this country and around the world. They are:

- Special agents and deputy marshals.
- Prosecutors, most of whom work in one of the ninety-four United States Attorney's Offices in all fifty states and the U.S. territories.
- Civil lawyers who represent the government in lawsuits, and are also spread all over the country.
- Analysts, scientists, paralegals, secretaries, clerks, mechanics, teachers, guards, and thousands of others who make the far-flung organization work.

That's the Justice Department. It is a diverse collection of people who all depend on the same thing—the thing I started to sense as a young law clerk sitting in Judge Walker's courtroom, a gift they received on joining the department. It is a gift they might not have noticed until the first time they stood up and identified themselves as a Justice employee and said something—whether in a courtroom, in a conference room, or at a cookout—and found that total strangers believed what they said next.

They were believed because, when they spoke, they weren't seen as Republicans or Democrats. They were seen as something separate and apart in American life—a group of people trying to do the right thing. I often describe that gift, which makes possible so much of the good they accomplish, as a reservoir of trust and credibility, a reservoir built for them, and filled one drop at a time by those who went before—most of whom they never knew. They were people who made sacrifices and kept promises to contribute to that reservoir. They were people who made mistakes, and admitted them. They were people who made hard calls without regard to politics or privilege, who sought the facts and applied them to the law.

The obligation of all Justice employees is to protect that reservoir, to pass it to those who follow, who will likely never meet or know them. The problem with reservoirs is that it takes tremendous time and effort to fill them, but one hole in a dam can drain them quickly. The protection of that reservoir requires vigilance, an unerring commitment to truth, and a recognition that the actions of one may affect the priceless gift that benefits all.

As a new federal prosecutor, painful lessons awaited me about my obligations to an institution—beyond any case—and to ensuring the whole truth was always told.

CHAPTER 2

THE FLY

The object of the superior [person] is truth.
CONFUCIUS

SPECIAL AGENT ALINA SACERIO-POLAK WAS eight months pregnant, so she instinctively shielded her torso as she covered the rear alley. The darkness of the October night offered some cover, but she still pressed herself tightly against a back corner of the brick Manhattan apartment building. She held her weapon in two hands, low-ready position, tight against the wall, watching the fire escape across the alley.

She heard the synchronized noise as her colleagues executing federal search warrants shouted "Police!" and banged on the doors of two identical rear apartments, one above the other, in classic drug dealer fashion: #8 was the retail outlet, #12 was the fortified stash. It was the late 1980s in New York City. Successful crack dealers were careful, and violent, even toward law enforcement. She tucked in tighter against the wall.

Seconds after the banging began, two men climbed out the retail drug apartment onto the fire escape. Sacerio-Polak and her partner shouted at them to stop. In reply, five shots rang out from above. She instantly pressed her cheek against the bricks, one eye far enough around the corner to search for the muzzle flashes above, and felt the sting of brick shards hitting her cheek as a round struck the brick by her eye. She returned fire, missing the shooter, but the drug dealer dropped his gun into the dark alley and began climbing behind his partner. She keyed her radio and alerted the agents stationed on the roof, who arrested the two.

The shooter, who claimed he was a salesman for a fictitious liquor store, was wearing thirty-one hundred dollars' worth of jewelry and had hundreds of dollars in cash in his pocket. He became one of the defendants in my first trial as a federal prosecutor, a five-defendant trial on charges of drug dealing, gun possession, and attempted murder of federal agents. It was exciting stuff, but the case had some serious problems—in the United States Attorney's Office for the Southern District of New York we called them "issues," a word that had a more optimistic ring to it.

One of those issues was "The Fly." He was the paid informant who had gone to apartment #8 and used federal taxpayer money to make "controlled buys" of crack vials in the days before the raid. The Fly, a Black man who was probably around forty, made his living by going places too dangerous for an undercover agent and pretending he was a drug user needing to score. It didn't require great acting ability. The Fly was a recovering addict and active methadone user, but he wouldn't be consuming the drugs he bought; they would become evidence in federal criminal investigations. Number 8 at 165 Edgecombe Avenue in Manhattan was a dangerous place controlled by a Jamaican drug gang; another customer had been raped there at gunpoint by one of the men who would later flee up the fire escape as his fellow gangster tried to kill federal agents. That danger was why the feds were trying to shut the operation down, and using the Fly to buy drugs.

The crack purchased by the Fly was evidence in my case, and he was to be a key witness. I met with him several times to prepare him to testify. The Fly, whose real name was Steve, insisted on being called the Fly or just "Fly," but I wasn't comfortable with either of those. He wasn't a great witness, but all I needed him to do was tell the jury about his trips to #8, after which he had initialed the crack vials he purchased, using the felt-tip marker the agents handed him when he returned to their car. And inside these heat-sealed bags with the evidence stickers were the vials. He recognized his initials. I offer them as evidence, Your Honor. Done.

The afternoon before the Fly's expected testimony, he reported to the United States Attorney's Office in lower Manhattan and waited in the seventh-floor reception area, sitting on the blue faux-leather couch until I returned from court to practice his testimony one last time. That morning, as was our habit during the trial, agents and I removed from the office's huge evidence vault the two metal carts holding the gun and drug evidence in the case. This day, we took only one of the carts to court. We wouldn't need the second cart, which held the Fly's crack evidence, until he testified. But I needed it to rehearse later with the Fly, so, as I left for court, the cart was in my office, guarded by a group of federal agents.

Then two things happened. First, each agent in the group assumed it was someone else's job to guard the drugs, as they wandered out of my office. Second, the Fly got lonely, stood up from the blue faux-leather couch, and did his own wandering, toward my office to find someone to chat with. That's how the Fly and the Fly's crack evidence came together without supervision. At that moment, the Fly decided to stop being a recovering addict; he stuffed the heat-sealed plastic bags into his pants and left the building, ending up high as a kite in a dumpy motel near LaGuardia Airport. But it would be days before I knew any of that.

Instead, what I learned after a long day in court was that drug evidence was missing from a cart in my office. The agents and I searched everywhere, as my throat began to tighten. Because I knew the history. I knew that a little more than a year earlier, shortly before I started as an Assistant United States Attorney in the Southern District of New York, another AUSA had been arrested for stealing drug evidence to use and to share with prostitutes living in his apartment. I knew that Rudy Giuliani, the United States Attorney who imagined for himself a bright public future, got very angry at that AUSA and ordered him handcuffed to a chair in the public lobby of the office, where the young man waited and sobbed until his court hearing was ready. That sobbing prosecutor with the missing drugs went to jail for three years. Rudy had asked for a twelve-year sentence.

I was having trouble swallowing when my supervisor told me Mr. Giuliani wanted to see me in his office that evening. Rudy and his deputy were there, and wanted to know what had happened to the drugs in my case. I explained that I had no idea. They said they wanted a sworn affidavit from me to that effect. Of course, I said, and returned to my office to type out the statement swearing that I had not stolen the drugs from my own case. I could type but no longer swallow.

My supervisors also told me to immediately tell the trial judge. The missing drugs were the basis for charges in the trial that was under way, I had talked about the informant's purchases in my opening statement, and the defense lawyers expected the informant to be a witness. They had to know. So, the next morning, I went to see the judge and told him and the defense lawyers the story, except for the ending, which I didn't yet know. That ending saved my career: agents found the Fly semiconscious in his Queens motel room, with the torn and empty and no-longer-heat-sealed evidence bags around him.

I didn't call the Fly as a witness, didn't offer any evidence of his controlled purchases of crack from #8, and dropped the charges connected to those purchases. The case survived the Fly.

But there were issues still to come.

Although the Fly didn't testify, a brave young woman did, describing how she was a regular customer at apartment #8—earlier in the same year as the federal raid—until she was raped at gunpoint by one of the defendants in my case, one of the two who fled out the window and up to the roof. Not the one who tried to murder the agents in the alley; the other one. After the assault, she ran from the apartment and called the police, who found the same two running the operation. The judge in my case wouldn't let her describe the sexual assault, because it was a state crime that couldn't be included in a federal indictment, but allowed her to tell the jury about the thriving drugstore and the two men who ran it.

And, of course, the federal agents testified about what they saw, heard, and found when they executed the search warrants that October night. The evidence—drugs of all kinds, guns, and hundreds of rounds of ammunition—went in fine. Then I got clever during my summation to the jury.

It was a throwaway line, really. How did the jury know the shooter was also a retail drug dealer? Because he had no job, wore thirty-one hundred dollars' worth of jewelry, and had hundreds of dollars in cash—all in small bills. "When you sell things for that [street] price," I told the jury, "you don't get big bills." I was pretty pleased with my first-ever summation.

I had practiced what I would say. Pacing back and forth at night in our tiny living room, I advocated to my pregnant wife playing juror on the brown corduroy couch.

"Very good," she said, "but why do you keep walking back and forth?"

"That's what lawyers do," I said. "You know, like on TV."

"Yeah, don't do that. You look like a giraffe in heat. You are six feet eight inches tall. You frighten people. Stand still. And stand back."

"Geez, that's kinda brutal."

"Yeah, I'm sorry. I love you so much. But don't move."

The next day, I got so comfortable on my stationary feet that I even ad-libbed when I noticed a juror sleeping in the front row as I spoke, during the part where I was recounting the defendants fleeing out the window onto the fire escape. Rather than say, as I had planned, that the defendant fired five shots at the agents, I said, "He looked down at them from the fire escape," paused, and then shouted, "BANG, BANG, BANG, BANG, BANG." The sleeper jolted awake.

Pleased that the case had gone in reasonably well, that the Fly, the drugs, and my career had all been, more or less, found, I relaxed in the courtroom as the jury retired to deliberate in the conference room behind the judge's bench. The lead case agent sidled over to me, told me I had done a good job, and asked if he could speak with me privately. My argument about the small bills in the defendant's pocket had brought to mind something he thought he should tell me.

After the defendants were arrested, but before my trial started, he had a crisis in an unrelated case: A group of drug dealers in Brooklyn kidnapped the mother of someone they believed had betrayed their gang, threatening to kill the woman unless the turncoat confessed. Another informant told the agents that he could take them to the kidnapped woman. But the informant wanted money first. It was after midnight on Saturday night. Where would they find money to pay the informant? My case agent went to his office, unlocked the evidence vault, and removed cash that had been seized in the raid on apartments #8 and #12, including the cash taken from the shooter's pocket on the roof. He used it to get information that allowed a SWAT team to rescue the kidnapped woman. Monday morning, he got replacement cash from agency funds and replaced what he had taken over the weekend.

As the agent sat in the courtroom and listened to me tell the jury that the small bills in the shooter's pocket meant he was a retail drug dealer, he realized he had a problem: He hadn't paid attention to the denominations of the bills he removed that weekend night, or the denominations of the replacement cash. He thought he had gotten the amounts right, but he couldn't say for sure that the money in the shooter's pocket was all ones, fives, and tens. Maybe it was now small bills because that's what he received from the office petty cash fund and replaced in the evidence envelope. Maybe it had been twenties before he touched it. Or fifties. He didn't know. So he told me about it.

I just wanted it to go away. I had survived the Fly. The jury was deliberating. Was it really worth blowing up the entire case over my throwaway argument? The guy was still an unemployed jewelry model with lots of cash in his pockets after climbing out of a drug apartment. Federal agents saw him try to kill them. He was guilty as hell. Who cared? My supervisor did. When I explained what the agent had told me, he instructed me to immediately go tell the trial judge. I could still argue that it didn't matter, that no action was required, but the court needed to know the truth, now.

I reluctantly marched from my office to the courthouse. The judge's courtroom assistant told me the judge was relaxing in his private office behind the bench, adjacent to the jury deliberation room. I should just go in. As I opened the door to the small, windowless office, I glanced toward his desk and immediately averted my eyes, apologizing for the interruption, and backing quickly from the room, stuttering, "Will come. Back. Your Honor." I hadn't seen much, mostly just his feet and the bottom hem of his judicial robe. But it was enough. The gray-haired, stern judge had been standing on his desk, in his long black robe, with one ear pressed to the air vent near the ceiling. I can't say for sure what he was doing. Maybe it had nothing to do with the jury room next door. Maybe it was about the temperature in his little office, or an annoying flying insect. He didn't say. I didn't ask. Back at the U.S Attorney's office, I told my supervisor what I had seen. "*That,* you can let go. But you still need to go back and tell him about the problem with the money. The arguments we make must be completely accurate."

I returned a short time later. The judge was sitting behind his desk. We both pretended I had not been there earlier. I explained the problem with the money and my argument, and asked him to hold a hearing where we would tell the defense lawyers and I would have a chance to argue the disclosure should make no difference. He cut me off quickly, ordering me to tell the defense lawyers. He was going to offer them the chance to halt jury deliberations, call the case agent to the stand to expose what he had done, and make new arguments about it to the jury, which would then continue deliberating. I had never heard of such a thing. He was making far too big a deal out of this. The small argument would make no difference. But the judge saw something I didn't yet see. As I started to protest, he cut me off and explained. Yes, the trial would still be fair without the unusual steps, but it wouldn't *appear* fair; the defendants would not have had the chance to argue something they believed was important. And the jury needed the whole truth from the Justice Department; they could decide what to make of it, but they had to get it.

Over my objection, the jury was recalled to the courtroom. The case agent testified about what he had done, admitted he broke the rules, and explained why he had done it. The lawyers attacked his credibility and told the jury they couldn't trust the government. The judge told the jury to start deliberating from the beginning, giving the case a fresh start, and considering all the evidence. The twelve New

Yorkers went back to their deliberation room, returning hours later to convict the defendants from whom money had been taken. It was a fair trial, in which the Department of Justice told the full story, despite the objection of a twenty-seven-year-old prosecutor trying his first case—learning an important lesson about telling the whole truth and nothing but the truth—and adding his first drops of water to the reservoir.

CHAPTER 3

HENRY

*If you see something that is not right, not fair, not just, you have a
moral obligation to do something about it.*
JOHN LEWIS

PATRICE AND I WERE NEVER GOING TO live in New
York. We met in college in Virginia and spent hours imagining our
future. It would not involve the New York area, where I had grown
up. She knew it well and wanted no part of it. After we were married,
we would live in Virginia, where we met and fell in love. While I
clerked for Judge Walker in Manhattan, she had already gone ahead
and was teaching at a public school outside Washington. I would never
ask her to live in the New York area. Until I watched Department of
Justice attorneys in court and called her.

"I know what I want to do with my life," I said.

"That's great," she replied. "What?"

I explained to her what a federal prosecutor was and what I was
so excited about.

"Sounds perfect for you," she said.

"And I want to do it here, in New York. It's the best place with the
best cases. Lots of energy. You can get a job up here. It'll be great."

There was a long pause. After many conversations, though, she concluded the Manhattan federal prosecutors' office really was the best opportunity for me. I told her it would only be a three-year commitment and then we would relocate. So, Patrice moved to New York and found a job, and we got married.

As newlyweds, we rented a small, one-bedroom apartment over a bike shop on the main street in Hoboken, New Jersey, just across the Hudson River from Manhattan. Patrice took a bus into the city every day and a subway to her office at Columbia University. I took a train to the World Trade Center and walked to my new job as a federal prosecutor in the office of Rudy Giuliani, the United States Attorney for the Southern District of New York. Rudy's tabloid-cover brashness and outsized personality excited the twenty-six-year-old me. It took me years to realize that a leadership culture focused entirely on the boss was not a healthy one, something the entire country would learn when Rudy's friend Donald Trump became president.

Patrice continued working until just before our first child was born. New York was a different city in 1988, one in which 1,842 human beings were murdered, then a record high, on the way to more record highs. During the hot summer of 1988, almost nine months pregnant, she was surrounded by a group of teens on the 1-2-3 subway line on Manhattan's West Side. As other passengers sat silently, the group taunted her for reading a book, poking her head to force her to look up, then snatched her book away, demanding money for its return. She stared at them, extending her hand, and said in her best classroom teacher voice, "Give . . . me . . . my . . . book." At that moment, the subway stopped at a station and the doors opened. Laughing, the young men spilled off the train, throwing her book back at her. The experience rattled her, and it scared me.

Like so many New York–area couples in the late 1980s, we decided to move away from the sense of disorder, and Patrice decided not to return to work after the baby was born. We found a three-bedroom, one-bath house to rent in Maplewood, New Jersey, fifteen miles west of Manhattan. It was actually half a house. The landlord, a widow with grown children, lived alone in the right half of the house. The left was ours. The rent was low enough, and the house close enough to the commuter train station, that we could live on my salary as a federal prosecutor and Patrice could stay home. We would live there for five years and have two of our kids before finally moving to Virginia.

When we moved to Maplewood, I was in the narcotics unit and uncomfortable with Henry Flete. He was technically guilty, but the whole thing didn't feel right to me. Henry had been arrested by the Drug Enforcement Administration and charged, along with a guy named Carlos Moreno, for a drug deal in the Bronx in which two DEA informants bought a kilo of cocaine from a major Colombian dealer. The dealer, who was the big fish, got away, leaving the little fish Moreno and a guppy named Henry Flete.

It all happened over a few days in May 1988. A DEA informant, working his first case since being arrested on drug charges—and hoping to convince the DEA to let him go—approached Flete near his home in the Bronx, not far from Yankee Stadium. The informant knew Flete's brother and believed Henry Flete knew people who dealt drugs, although he had never worked with him. Speaking Spanish, the informant chatted for a long time with Flete, before finally saying he was looking to find a source for cocaine. After some conversation, Flete agreed to try to find someone. The next day, on the same street, Flete introduced a Colombian to the informant. With Flete standing nearby, the Colombian and the informant agreed to do the deal for a kilo of cocaine at a White Castle burger restaurant off the Cross Bronx Expressway. That was it for Henry. He made the introduction and walked away.

Near the White Castle the next day, Carlos Moreno waited with the kilo of 96 percent pure cocaine in a brown zippered case as the Colombian and the informant met. The informant said he wanted to examine the drugs before delivering them to his boss, who would have the money. The informant and the Colombian drove from the restaurant parking lot, picked up Moreno, and parked around the corner. From the back seat, Moreno unzipped the case and handed over a brown paper bag holding the kilo. The informant, in plain view of Moreno and the Colombian, pushed a key through the kilo's wrapper, withdrawing it covered in white powder. The informant said he was satisfied, and directed the Colombian to drive them to where his "boss"—another DEA informant—was waiting. The Colombian stayed in his car as Moreno and the first informant got into the second informant's car. There, they replayed the inspection process, with the "boss" pushing his own keys through the kilo's wrapping to inspect it. Satisfied, the boss got out, supposedly to retrieve the purchase money from the trunk, which was a signal to waiting DEA agents. As the arrest team swooped in, Moreno threw the kilo into the front seat. He was arrested. The Colombian dealer drove off and they lost him. But the DEA found and arrested Flete shortly afterward.

Less than a year into my career as a federal prosecutor, I inherited the case after it had been charged. My job was to handle the trial of Carlos Moreno and Henry Flete on conspiracy and drug possession charges. I thought the evidence showed that Moreno was a paid courier for the Colombian, deeply involved in the operation. He would not have been walking around the streets of the Bronx with a kilo of pure coke otherwise. The jury agreed, despite Moreno's testimony at trial that he had no idea it was cocaine in the package, had never heard there was cocaine in his hometown of Cali, Colombia, and was only delivering a package for a powerful fellow Colombian for a modest fee.

Flete was a harder case. There was no evidence he was part of an ongoing drug organization. He had never been in trouble before. A guy who knew his brother had chatted him up and asked him to find him a drug dealer. That conversation was not recorded, so we didn't know how the informant approached him. Flete knew a dealer, so he made the introduction, although the dealer didn't trust Flete to be involved in the deal. Flete shouldn't have done that, because it is a crime to assist a drug deal. But given the amount of drugs in the case, he was headed to jail for a five-year mandatory sentence. That didn't feel right to me.

After learning the details of the case, I went to my narcotics unit supervisors and explained that I was uncomfortable prosecuting Flete. He seemed like a sad sack who didn't deserve a five-year hit. They asked me whether the evidence was legally sufficient. Yes, I replied. Flete took a step to assist what he knew would be a drug deal; in the eyes of the law, he participated in a cocaine conspiracy, even though we had no proof he got money for it, and he didn't participate in the actual transaction. He knew the stranger on the street was looking for drugs and he introduced him to a drug dealer. But it still doesn't feel right, I added. I'd like to drop the case against Flete. They refused, explaining that DEA would be very unhappy with that because it was important to send a message that nobody should be helping the drug trade. Yeah, I answered, but for five years in federal prison? He'll get the full five because he has nobody to cooperate against to earn a sentence reduction. Try the case, they told me. This is your job. Argue the government's case. Nobody added that our boss, Rudy Giuliani, was about to run for mayor as a tough-on-crime candidate, so we wouldn't be dismissing drug cases in the Bronx. But they didn't need to; Rudy's ambition pervaded the place. I said I understood and would try the case.

As instructed, I argued to the jury that the evidence established guilt. Flete didn't offer a defense, but Moreno took the stand and lied, so I went after him aggressively. I don't know what the jury read in me, but they acquitted Flete, who went free. Moreno served five years. And I asked to be transferred out of the narcotics unit.

I should have refused to try Henry Flete and insisted my supervisors drop the case or find another prosecutor to handle it. But I didn't have the guts—or realize how important it was to the Department of Justice that I not do things I didn't fully believe in. Years later, when I became the United States Attorney, the job Giuliani had when I was that young narcotics prosecutor, I gave each Assistant United States Attorney a framed certificate. It held words of direction and inspiration from one of my predecessors in the job, Whitney North Seymour Jr. In 1973, with Watergate starting to stain the Department of Justice, he told his assistant attorneys:

> To be an Assistant United States Attorney for the Southern
> District of New York requires commitment to absolute
> integrity and fair play; to candor and fairness in dealing with
> adversaries and the courts; to careful preparation, not making
> any assumptions or leaving anything to chance; and never
> proceeding in a case unless convinced of the correctness of
> one's position or the guilt of the accused.

Lawyers for the Justice Department are not representing a client in the normal sense of that word. I would learn from experience that a lawyer for a private client has an ethical obligation to make the best argument for the client; private lawyers are not stewards of an institution in the same way. But as a federal prosecutor, I had a responsibility beyond any case or witness or colleague, because my client wasn't in the courtroom. My client was a concept, one at the heart of our democracy: justice.

My first year as a federal prosecutor wasn't all problems and ethical dilemmas. There were some cases that were just kind of cool, and deepened my love for the work, like the dental floss escape of a mysterious criminal from the seventh floor of the Manhattan federal prison.

The real estate broker called the cops because it was so strange. The thirty-year-old guy who said he was a U.S. government employee named Michael Anderson didn't seem right. He was vague about which agency he worked for and was interested in buying only a certain kind of luxury apartment—the top floor of a building on Manhattan's East Side. She called the cops, who called the FBI's Joint Terrorism Task Force, which introduced undercover special agents to the process. "Anderson" told the agents, posing as the broker's associates, that he worked for the United States Department of Defense "on a joint task force with the State Department."

The agents arrested Anderson for impersonating a federal officer and searched his briefcase. They found an astonishing array of weaponry: an M-11 nine-millimeter semiautomatic pistol containing a magazine loaded with ten rounds; a silencer for the gun; a knife; smoke grenades; a garrote; and bottles of strychnine and chloroform; along with rubber gloves, sponges, and a needle syringe. The briefcase also held floor plans for apartments in the building. In his Pennsylvania rental home, the FBI found components for bombs, chemical weapons, and formulas for homemade nerve gas. He was an Iranian national illegally in the country after overstaying a student visa. The FBI didn't know what this guy was up to, only that it was really bad, and his claim that he had been coerced into acting for the Iranian government made no sense.

As I prepared the case for trial, the defendant was ordered held without bail at the twelve-story maximum-security federal prison next to my office and the federal courthouse in lower Manhattan. Just yards from my office window, the Iranian and his two drug-dealer cellmates were working hard in their seventh-floor cell. First, they had to spend hours pressing on the thick Plexiglas with the heating element of the iron they stole from the laundry, using it as the world's slowest blowtorch to melt a human-sized square in the cell window. But that process was quick compared with making the rope. To do that, they stole boxes of dental floss, weaving the long strands night after night, until they had many yards of long, thin, but unbreakable rope. Then they were ready to go.

Late one night, they pushed the melted window out and tied one end of the dental floss rope to the cell plumbing, pitching the rest out and down the side of the prison. It was all in place: window, rope, and a critical third ingredient—gloves. The rope was impossibly strong and dangerously thin, but they stole two pairs of work gloves inside the prison—one each for the drug dealers; two for the Iranian, because it was his plan.

There was some kind of panic in the cell as the three made their escape. The drug dealers, each with their single glove, managed to slide down the rope, landing on the roof of an electrical substation four floors below. But the Iranian went out barehanded; his gloves were found on his bed. He started sliding down the brilliant white rope without them. The recovered dental floss rope became pink about ten feet down, and then dark red with his blood the rest of the way, until he could stand the pain no more and let go. He fell hard on the substation roof, hurting an ankle. He could not join the drug dealers in their scramble over the concertina barbed wire at the edge of the rooftop and down to the street, where they were captured by deputy United States marshals. Instead, he was stuck on the substation roof, bleeding profusely from tendon-shearing cuts to both hands, and hopping with a bum ankle.

Marshals soon raised a mechanical cherry picker to the roof level to retrieve the third escapee. As the two deputy U.S. marshals leveled weapons at him, the Iranian warned them not to come any closer, declaring that the small vial he was holding in his bloody hand contained strychnine, which he would swallow if they attempted to capture him. In a reply that soon became famous in the New York federal law enforcement community, Deputy U.S. Marshal John Cuff— his real name—replied, "Hey, you gotta do what you gotta do." With that, he and his partner jumped on the Iranian as he quickly tried to swallow the vial, forcing his mouth open and recovering what would turn out to be a glass vial containing actual strychnine.

The mysterious Iranian was so badly injured that he was taken to a lower Manhattan hospital for surgical repair of his hands. There, he was watched over by two contract guards, retired law enforcement officers hired by the Marshals Service to sit in his room around the clock. As both contract guards slept soundly in chairs in his room, the Iranian slipped out of the hospital, barefoot in sweatpants and a T-shirt. Enraged, the United States marshal himself confronted the guards, who said the Iranian must have drugged them. The chief marshal ordered them to the emergency room to have their stomachs pumped. The pumping produced only orange juice and coffee, although apparently not enough coffee.

The Iranian disappeared for three days. We got a break when he called an acquaintance to arrange a Western Union money transfer. As the fugitive walked into a Manhattan Western Union office to retrieve his money, the employees all dove behind the counter and an FBI SWAT team captured him, for the third and last time. He was dirty, with a variety of cuts and bruises around his face and neck. He seemed almost relieved to be captured this time, explaining that he had fled to a high-crime area of upper Manhattan after leaving the hospital. There, he was mugged twice and beaten each time because he had no money for the robbers. New York in 1988 was no place for shoeless and penniless foreign fugitives.

Shortly before his trial, Iranian-backed terrorists in Lebanon captured, tortured, and executed a United States Marine colonel assigned to a United Nations peacekeeping mission, prompting the Iranian's lawyer to seek a postponement of the Manhattan trial. The judge denied the motion, saying, "If we delay this trial until terrorists stop killing innocent Americans, we will never have it." The jury deliberated for six minutes before returning a verdict of guilty on five counts, and he was sentenced to a long prison term, from which he did not escape. Federal prisons started handing out dental floss in precut pieces. And my dentist had me retell the story during every checkup.

I came to love the work, but my first year as a fed taught me that I owed a duty to something above any case or embarrassment. As a federal prosecutor, I wasn't a lawyer hired to win a case. I represented the principle of justice and was obligated to figure out the right thing to do, and then advocate for that, not victory. In trying Henry Flete, I had violated the spirit of that creed and participated in something that didn't feel right. I didn't have the backbone to stand up for the values that drew me to the Department of Justice. It was a painful lesson, one I would never forget. There were others ahead.

CHAPTER 4

LIARS

The more cunning a man is, the less he suspects he will be
caught in a simple thing.
FYODOR DOSTOEVSKY

EVERYBODY LIES, nearly every day. When you are asked by a colleague, "Hey, how's it goin'?" you always answer, "Great, thanks," even when it is not. You check a box saying you read the terms and conditions of the new app so you can get the darn thing started. You tell your sister you like her new tattoo. Everybody lies.

Our leaders do, and they always have. In many ways, we insist that they mislead us. After a candidate wins the nomination of a political party, we speak of the candidate needing to "tack to the middle" to attract more voters. Wait, what? Isn't that a way of saying we expect the candidate, having convinced primary voters he believes something, to convince general election voters he actually believes something else? Doesn't that mean he is lying to somebody?

But in a pluralistic democracy, we accept that kind of lying as a necessary evil. One of our national saints, Abraham Lincoln, was elected president in 1860 after some voters concluded he would abolish slavery and other voters decided he would merely limit its expansion into new states. Those both can't be true. He allowed both sides to believe what they wanted, got elected, and saved our nation.

Donald Trump as president took lying to another level. Yes, he lied more often and about more things than any leader in our history, but he and his followers also did something profoundly dangerous: they attacked the idea that truth exists, that it can be found. This country's touchstone has long been the idea that truth is a real thing, and that it must be sought and spoken. We have always understood that leaders make false statements, but we have never stopped measuring them against the touchstone. George Bush spoke falsely when he said there were weapons of mass destruction in Iraq; Barack Obama spoke falsely when he said if you like your doctor you can keep your doctor. Then both men spent the remainder of their time in office, and maybe the rest of their lives, explaining themselves—what they meant, what they thought, why they said it. They did that because, despite our many flaws as a nation, we hold to the idea that truth exists and that it matters. Or at least we once did.

Our founders created systems of government and justice designed to have the best chance of finding truth, by crashing human interests against each other. In courtrooms we argue and cross-examine and challenge recollections and interpretations and perspectives, to arrive at truth. The justice system, in particular, depends upon our shared belief that truth can be found to a high degree of confidence, a degree high enough that we deprive people of their liberty—and sometimes their lives, in cases that are increasingly rare, thankfully—based on the truth we find. The system rejects the notion that truth is all relative—my perspective, your perspective, who's to say? Yes, there are perspectives and beliefs that represent our personal "truths," but there are also facts that are verifiable or falsifiable—the truth.

Our justice system is designed to find the answers, which are not about perspective. And to get to that answer, those who participate in the system must themselves offer an honest account. The whole design rests upon oaths and promises, solemn commitments to recount what was really seen or heard. If that slips away, if participants in the justice system adopt the Trump model—truth is whatever I say it is—then justice is lost. To protect justice, liars must be held accountable.

It was a crime for the record books, something out of *Mission: Impossible,* executed in broad daylight on a busy Manhattan block with no witnesses. One October morning, just as business in Manhattan's busy fur district was getting started for the day, a team of masked gunmen forced their way into a fur dealership on the third floor of a building at 208 West Twenty-ninth Street, between Seventh and Eighth Avenues. The robbers, pushing empty canvas laundry carts, handcuffed and blindfolded the owner and his foreman and forced them to lie on the ground as they cleaned out the place. The victims could hear the cart wheels scraping the floor as the robbers hauled the heavy inventory of minks and foxes. The robbers then moved the two captives into the empty vault, where they left them handcuffed, gagged, and blindfolded with heavy tape, escaping with 121 fur coats and 8,180 fur pelts. A short time later, the victims managed to get the tape from their mouths and shout for help. Workers from an adjacent construction business rescued them, but the robbers had disappeared into thin air with their incredible haul.

It was so good that it seemed too good. The insurance company, which was asked to reimburse the owner for the loss, got suspicious and contacted the FBI. Of course, that likely wouldn't go anywhere. Maybe it seemed impossible for the robbers to have gotten away without anyone seeing them, but proving beyond a reasonable doubt that something didn't happen is a tall order. The FBI would likely take a look and then send it back to the insurance company to fight about in civil litigation.

But the *Mission: Impossible* case got assigned to a special agent with the New York FBI's Major Theft Squad. He was a cynical, smart, darkly funny former Philadelphia trial attorney who claimed to have come into the FBI at an earlier time, "when standards were low." Unmarried and a runner, he also smoked, drank, and avoided long-term relationships. He did not, however, avoid work and would not let go if something smelled odd. He didn't like the smell of the fur "robbery" and convinced my supervisors at the Manhattan U.S. Attorney's Office to open an investigation and assign it to me.

After we dug into the case, we were surprised when the owner of the "victim" fur business offered to testify before the grand jury that had just begun investigating. He came to the lower Manhattan courthouse, into the modified courtroom used by the grand jury, and raised his right hand, promising to tell the truth and nothing but the truth, so help him God. His lawyer wasn't allowed in the room, nor were the FBI agents. It was me, him, a court reporter to make a transcript, and the grand jurors.

A federal grand jury is a body made up of twenty-three citizens who hear evidence from the government about possible criminal cases. They are chosen by a federal judge from the pool of people called for jury duty, but serve in secret, without a judge present, deciding—usually after hearing only the prosecution's side of a story—whether someone should be indicted, that is, formally accused of a crime. To reach that decision, they frequently investigate, having prosecutors issue subpoenas on their behalf to bring witnesses and documents to them. If someone being investigated offers to testify, they almost always grant the request.

Once the grand jury members gather the evidence they think relevant, they decide whether a prosecution should begin with an indictment. If at least twelve members of the grand jury vote to indict someone, using the standard of "probable cause"—whether it's probable that the person did it—the case will then go to court. There, the government must prove guilt to a much higher standard—beyond a reasonable doubt—and a trial jury must be unanimous before it may find someone guilty. The grand jury is one of the oldest features of Western law, created in England hundreds of years ago to limit the power of the king. The idea was that only other citizens could accuse someone of a serious crime. Our founders borrowed it from English law and made it an important part of the United States Constitution.

It is a big deal to lie during a federal investigation, whether to a grand jury or an FBI agent. That's because the system rests on a bit of a myth—that you have no choice but to tell the truth and provide your evidence. In reality, justice is an honor system; the government really can't always tell when people are lying or hiding documents. So, when they *are* able to prove it, they simply must punish people for lying, a message to everyone. People must fear the consequences of lying in the justice system or the system can't work.

There was once a time when most people worried about going to hell if they violated an oath taken in the name of God—when "so help me God" put the fear of eternal damnation in a witness. That divine deterrence has slipped away from our modern cultures. In its place, people must fear going to jail. People must fear having their name forever associated with a criminal act if we are to have a nation under the rule of law.

The fur guy came before the grand jury and spent hours telling his detailed story about the robbery. If that wasn't true, then, to protect the institution of justice and reinforce a culture of truth-telling, he had to be prosecuted. And it certainly didn't seem true.

We had some decent motive proof. We could establish that in the weeks leading up to the robbery, the fur company owner had lost a major sale to a prominent national retail fur store chain, a loss he told others had hurt his little company "terribly." We could establish that he told his landlord he was deeply in debt and couldn't pay the rent, which didn't matter because, he said, the company would likely be out of business by the beginning of October. We could prove the company moved some furs out of its facility in the week before the robbery and also shipped fur to its Florida facility. But it wasn't so much fur that the company couldn't explain it as normal business activity. We could show from alarm records that the owner had done something unusual the night before the robbery. The business always closed at about four thirty, but that night, after all the employees left and the alarm was armed at its usual time, the owner returned, disarmed the alarm, and stayed for a couple of hours.

Our biggest problem was that we couldn't find the allegedly stolen furs or financial evidence of the money made from secretly selling them after a fake robbery. There was no doubt the company had a real inventory of furs. If the robbery was a fake, the furs went someplace; we just couldn't show where. We could argue the company sold slightly more furs after the robbery than it should have been able to, but it wasn't a home run. Our inability to find the furs might be a reasonable doubt.

After hearing evidence, the grand jury thought the man's testimony was probably a lie. So they indicted the company owner and his foreman. The case was going to come down to whether we could convince a trial jury that the robbery simply couldn't have happened that October morning and that the fur company owner and his foreman were lying. But if the jury was left with a doubt based in reason, they would walk. So, we set out to narrow the window available to the "robbers" that morning, until there was not even a crack they could have slipped through.

There were no video cameras anywhere in the building, but alarm company records showed that the fur boss and his foreman entered their third-floor space at 6:48 that morning. NYPD records established that their rescuers called 911 at 7:26 A.M. The owner had testified in the grand jury that the five robbers entered the space at least several minutes after he disarmed the alarm, took some time to force entry, and took more time to get the vault open after the owner struggled to remember the combination. The victims said they waited an additional five minutes before shouting for help. One robber stayed with each victim throughout the robbery, leaving three robbers to do the job, each then responsible for moving hundreds of pounds of furs. That meant the robbers had about twenty minutes—tops—to remove the entire inventory from the third floor to the street, which would require some kind of wheeled equipment, like the laundry carts the victims said they saw.

But nobody else saw them, when they should have. An employee of the construction firm that shared the third floor with the fur company unlocked the building's front door at 6:30 A.M. and rode the sole passenger elevator to the third floor. He walked to the construction business, located just across the hall from the fur company. The construction company door was already open to the hall; one of his coworkers was already there. For the rest of the morning, the two men left the door to the hall wide open for ventilation purposes.

The owner of a flower company on the fifth floor parked in front at approximately 6:30 A.M. and walked down the block to a nearby flower market. He passed his employee coming the other way, headed to work. That employee recalled that at around 6:45 A.M., after passing his boss, he entered the building and rode the passenger elevator to the fifth floor. Because the only other elevator, a freight elevator, was still locked off by steel gates for the night, he began assembling trays of flowers to put in the passenger elevator.

At 6:48 A.M., the fur company owner and his foreman entered their business and turned off the alarm. At 6:50, the flower company employee called the passenger elevator to the fifth floor and held it there as he loaded flower trays. At 6:55, his boss returned from the flower market and saw from the lighted numbers atop the lobby elevator door that the elevator was on the fifth floor. He turned and entered the building's internal staircase, which could be entered only from the lobby. He walked up to the fifth floor.

From 6:50 to 7:15, the flower company employee made two trips to the lobby with flower arrangements, using the passenger elevator. He left the first load in the lobby as he returned upstairs. The flowers nearly filled the small lobby. At 7:10, the building custodian entered the lobby. He waited for the passenger elevator to descend and then helped unload flowers into the lobby. He joined the flower company employee for a ride back up to the fifth floor, where the custodian entered the building manager's office to have breakfast. At 7:15, the flower guy returned to the lobby and spent five minutes moving the flowers into the van his boss had parked in front earlier. His boss joined him at 7:20 A.M. and they drove away to begin the day's deliveries. Across the street sat a parking lot attendant in a small hut with windows on all sides. He saw nothing unusual that morning.

At about 7:20 A.M., another employee of the third-floor construction business—the one directly across the hall from the fur company—entered the building, took the elevator to the third floor, walked a step past the fur company's door, then turned sharply into the open door of his employer across the hall. He had just started to have some coffee when he heard a sound and stepped into the hall to investigate. He heard the fur owner and his foreman shouting for help and alerted his co-workers. They called 911 at 7:26 A.M. and entered the fur business, rescuing the victims from the vault.

They found the foreman on the floor, handcuffed behind his back, with tape around his legs, eyes, and mouth. He had used the leg of a sawhorse table in the vault to scrape the tape from his mouth. The fur company owner was handcuffed differently. He was standing, with his hands cuffed in front of him, around a pole in the large walk-in vault. His hands were at the same level as his face, allowing him to peel off the tape and yell for help. He said the robbers had tried to handcuff his hands behind his back but found him too muscular; they instead handcuffed him in front, but warned him not to remove the mouth tape, saying they would be waiting outside. The robbers did not close the vault door when they left. And as fast as they must have been working, the robbers did some selective shopping in the vault, leaving behind two old mink coats and one brown leather coat.

At 7:55 A.M., the custodian, unaware of the commotion two floors below, left the building manager's office, walking down the fifth-floor hallway to the freight elevator. He found it locked at the fifth floor, where he had left it the night before. He unlocked and rode the freight elevator to the first floor, where he unlocked the steel gates closing off the rear staircase and the freight entrance to the building.

The responding NYPD officers and the building manager searched the entire building, including the one vacant office space, and found no furs or evidence of robbers.

I argued to the jury that, in addition to the fact that nobody in or around the building that morning saw or heard anything unusual, the evidence established that the two elevators—one locked on the fifth floor and the other almost continuously in use between 6:40 and 7:26 A.M.—could not have been used by five men with laundry carts to move more than two thousand pounds of furs. The stairs, which were either locked or similarly trafficked that morning, were also unavailable. On top of that, the gang of robbers and their heavy booty could not have moved past the open door of the construction business across the hall. The construction company employees had been able to hear the muffled cries coming from inside the fur company, but heard no other movement.

We felt good about our case. But "beyond a reasonable doubt" is a heavy burden—as it should be—and we needed some way to make this real for the jury. Using the books and records of the fur company, the FBI was able to establish what coats and fur pelts should have been in the vault that morning. Armed with that information, the Bureau went to furriers all over New York and borrowed enough furs to duplicate what was allegedly stolen that October morning.

Late at night before the final day of trial, a large, unmarked white truck pulled up on Pearl Street in Manhattan, parking outside the side entrance to the courthouse. FBI agents holding shotguns guarded the truck, as other agents carried racks of furs up to the courtroom. There, with the court's permission, agents removed the spectator benches from the courtroom, to make space for the furs. Agents spent the rest of the night guarding the furs, waiting for the jury.

When the jury walked into court that final morning, there was no room for spectators. The courtroom was a sea of minks and foxes, furs that a group of five robbers supposedly moved out the door, through the hall, down three flights of stairs, through a lobby jammed with flowers, and out the front door of 208 West Twenty-ninth Street, in less than twenty minutes and without being seen. In a valiant effort, a defense lawyer equipped himself with leather shoulder straps that furriers use to carry fur pelts. These look like thick belts with a large sharp hook at each end. He had a paralegal load him up with 1,365 pelts on the four hooks in forty-two seconds. It was impressive, but you could almost hear the poor man's spine compressing as he stood there with a pained grin on his face. I reminded the jury that he had not taken a step, for good reason: "The front line of the New York Giants with that stuff on their shoulders could not walk out the front door of the business, much less go down the hall and sneak past. . . .

And if they were using the hooks that have been shown you, why did they bring the laundry carts?"

We had proven that the mission really was impossible. The jury agreed, returning a unanimous verdict finding the defendants guilty of perjury and fraud. They did not get the insurance money. The fur company foreman by that time had developed a brain tumor, so I agreed to a sentence of probation. The boss went to jail for three years. Liars must be held accountable.

I didn't prosecute many drug cases during my brief stint in the narcotics unit at the United States Attorney's Office in Manhattan. But I held on to a trial that grew out of the Drug Enforcement Administration's effort to stop the movement of large quantities of heroin from West Africa to New York. The international drug trade was more interesting than dealers at White Castles in the Bronx, but I kept the trial mostly because the case agent was warm and funny, with an infectious laugh. He sat two seats to my left at the government's courtroom table. The seat between us was reserved for the one essential member of our trial team, the DEA interpreter who spoke the tribal languages of Ghana and who would guide me to an unforgettable courtroom confrontation with a very sympathetic liar.

The interpreter whispered in my left ear. "That's the Ashanti name given to every boy born on a Thursday." Sometimes liars make big mistakes. This was a big mistake. A man from the Bronx was on trial for narcotics trafficking, accused of being part of a ring of heroin dealers from the West African nation of Ghana who were moving kilos of heroin to the New York area on commercial flights. The key evidence consisted of tapes made through a court-ordered wiretap, in which the defendant could be heard arranging deals. We knew it was him because his partner in the heroin operation testified against him, people who knew him well identified his voice on the tapes, and the key calls were made from his home phone.

But his wife was on the witness stand, explaining to the jury that she knew it wasn't her husband on the wiretap tapes the DEA had made because the men on the tape were speaking in the Ashanti tribal dialect. A man who lived in an apartment above them had no phone, she said, and would come use theirs from time to time. He was from Ghana, but Ashanti. She and her husband, she said, were Ga people, speakers of an entirely different Ghanaian tribal language. Neither of them spoke a word of Ashanti, so that couldn't be him on the tapes. It must be the neighbor.

Despite the strong evidence we presented, I had a sinking feeling, sitting at the government's courtroom table, watching this nice-looking person explain to the jury that we had the wrong man. How was I going to cross-examine her? Could I yell "Look out behind you!" in Ashanti and watch her turn her head? But I don't speak Ashanti, or Ga.

And then she made a mistake. In an apparent effort to generate sympathy, the defense lawyer asked if she had any children. She replied, "Yes, one."

"And what's his name?"

"He's a junior, named for my husband."

"Do you call him by a nickname?"

"Yes, Yaw."

"And how old is Yaw?"

"He's six."

As the lawyer moved on to other questions about the family's relocation to America, the government interpreter who had translated the wiretap tapes on which the case was based leaned to my left ear.

She was of Ghanaian ancestry. She had lived there. She knew the tribal traditions and spoke the tribal languages. "The Ashanti give their children second names based on their day of birth. It's to mark the day God decided to give this child to the world. The Ga don't do anything like that. Never."

The defense lawyer finished. I was on my feet, my heart pounding, trying not to blow this. I began with some innocuous questions, to try to relax the witness, and me. And then I hit it.

"Ma'am, you mentioned your son, who you call Yaw. When was he born?"

"January twenty-first, 1982." I had no idea what day of the week that was but pressed on. It was worth a gamble.

"What day of the week was that?" Her eyes widened just a tiny bit. She saw me. She knew she had made a big mistake.

"It was the twenty-first."

"Yes, ma'am, you said that. But what day of the week was it?"

"I don't remember. It was cold."

"Yes, ma'am, it was January, as you said. But what day of the week?" I felt like I could push here. A mother who had her only child six years ago would know the day of the week.

"I don't remember."

"Was it a weekend? Weekday?

"I don't remember."

"Is Yaw your only child?"

"Yes."

"And you still have no idea what day of the week you gave birth for the only time in your life?"

"I don't."

"Where did you get the nickname 'Yaw'?"

"I think we heard it on the subway and it was just a name we liked."

That made me feel better about my gamble, so I went for it, even though, in the ancient days before internet searches or cell phones, I didn't have a 1982 calendar to check. But it had to be a Thursday.

"Ma'am, January twenty-first, 1982, was a Thursday, wasn't it?"

"I don't know."

"You and your husband are Ashanti, aren't you?"

"No."

"And the Ashanti people give second names to their children based on their day of birth?"

"I wouldn't know."

"The Ga people don't do that, right?"

"That's correct. We don't."

"Yaw is the Ashanti name for a boy born on a Thursday?"

"I have no idea."

"You named him Yaw because he was born on a Thursday, right?"

"No. I don't know what day he was born."

"You and your husband both speak Ashanti and that's your husband on the tapes, isn't it?"

"No, that's not true."

"I have nothing further, Your Honor."

I ended my cross-examination and sat down, heart pounding. The judge said he would take a five-minute recess. It was going to be close. I walked calmly out of the courtroom, turned the hallway corner away from spectators, and began running. I ran down the stairs to the third floor of the Thurgood Marshall United States Courthouse. I sprinted across the pedestrian bridge to the U.S. Attorney's Office, and straight to the office of the oldest Assistant United States Attorney I knew. I remembered that she had years, decades really, of red hardbound calendar diaries lined up on her bookshelves, the years written in white on the spines. She wasn't there. I grabbed 1982 off the shelf and slapped the pages to January 21. Thursday. Still holding her book, I ran back, slowing to a walk when I came near the courtroom door, gasping for air.

The judge took the bench. I rose, holding the 1982 book. I was still having trouble breathing. "Your Honor, I ask that the Court take judicial notice"—I paused to grab more air—"that January twenty-first, 1982, was"—pause, gulp, pause—"a Thursday."

The judge looked down at me from the bench. He wasn't out of breath, but took his own pause, then, very slowly, said, "I know, Mr. Comey, I checked."

I sat down. This drug dealer was going to jail. After his wife's brazen lying, I struggled with whether to charge her with perjury. Yes, the entire system fails if witnesses lie without consequence, but her husband was going to jail for many years and a case against her was unappealing. She lied to try to save him, and a jury would be reluctant—as I was—to make a young boy an orphan. It just wasn't worth doing. But other cases would be different, and not about desperate spouses and six-year-olds. They would involve powerful liars, some with a president for an ally. If the truth was to remain at the center of our justice system, those were the cases that had to be pursued.

CHAPTER 5

BUGS

[T]he passions of [humans] will not conform to the dictates of
reason and justice without constraint.
ALEXANDER HAMILTON

THERE IS A LOT OF FREE TIME IN organized crime. In
warmer weather, the mobsters would stand in front of their Manhattan jewelry-district business to make it easier for the New York area's
high-end burglars and armed robbers to find them, to see what they
wanted to buy or commission to be stolen. They might retreat inside
to talk, but they liked to stand in front, whispering to each other.
In colder weather, though, they passed the time inside, often on the
phone—a landline, if such a thing can be imagined in our wireless
world—and there was our chance.

It is very hard to get permission to wiretap someone's phone or
plant a bug in their car or home or office. And it should be, because
there is little the government can do—at least, there wasn't before we
all started carrying our entire lives with us on smartphones—that
more directly implicates core constitutional rights. In a criminal case,
it requires a federal prosecutor to prepare a lengthy sworn statement
that establishes probable cause to believe the proposed target of the

surveillance is committing serious federal crimes, using a particular phone or place to commit those crimes, and that we have tried all other possible less-intrusive investigative techniques to get evidence without wiretapping. In the case of the jewelry-district mobsters, we had tried sending informants in to talk to them and tape the conversations, but they were very guarded. For three years, agents conducted surveillance, but pictures of criminals standing together are of limited use. We had subpoenaed phone records and bank records and credit records, but all of it just confirmed something sketchy was going on; no piece of paper reveals what they are planning, who they are hurting, where the danger is. There was no good substitute for getting permission to hear what they were saying on the phone.

But to get to hear it, I first had to draft the long application, including the sworn affidavit laying out the evidence we had so far, have that reviewed by my supervisors, then send it to Washington for approval. Then, and only then, could I go show it to a judge and seek a court order. But the case agent and I had to personally show it to the judge, and swear that what we said was complete, true, and accurate. If the judge agreed, she would issue an order good for thirty days of listening, but require me to file with the court every ten days a report on the progress of the wiretap and our compliance with the standard conditions of minimization.

The rules were clear that agents could not listen to every call; they could listen to only the first few seconds of a call and then had to turn off the monitoring equipment and recorder unless they concluded—and documented in writing—that the call was "pertinent," meaning it was likely to be criminal and within the authority of the wiretap order. Calls with the mobster's children, or counsel, or priest, or even golf buddy could not be listened to or recorded unless there was good reason to believe the kids, lawyers, clergy, or golfers were part of the conspiracy. And the basis for listening to any such call would have to be explained to the judge every ten days.

It was a pain in the neck, and FBI agents—sitting in a "wire room" at the FBI, where the phone company routed duplicate phone lines— lived in fear of making a mistake, such as listening too long or not listening long enough. Sometimes they couldn't believe their ears.

The mobsters thought they were safe up there. Gambino family boss John Gotti used the Ravenite Social Club on Mulberry Street, in Manhattan's Little Italy, as his headquarters. But he knew that the feds knew that, and that they might try to get court orders to listen to his conversations. So he made them very hard to hear. For most conversations, he took it outside, going on "walk-talks" around the neighborhood, even whispering in the ear of his conversation partner, outside. He appeared to have internalized the life lessons of family founder Carlo Gambino, who, it was said, died a free man of natural causes because he talked about family business with only a few trusted underlings, and then only outdoors when whispering.

But Gotti and his number two, family underboss Salvatore "Sammy the Bull" Gravano, had a secret. They didn't want to go outside all the time. And they didn't need to, because they had a safe place. It took the FBI, working with federal prosecutors from the Eastern District of New York—a different office from mine—a long time to figure it out. Agents could tell from the court-ordered bugs around the Mafia headquarters that the boss and underboss were leaving the club but not emerging onto the street. Where were they going? Gravano explained to me during his 1993 testimony in a Mafia case—*United States v. John Gambino*—where we used the evidence collected by our colleagues:

"Was there another location besides the street at the Ravenite that you considered a safe place from electronic interception?"

"Yes."

"Where was that?"

"It was, there was an apartment upstairs. There was a made member who died. His wife still had this apartment. She was about eighty years old. She was always home. We felt that that was a secure location, and occasionally we would go through the back door up the staircase, go into this apartment, and have some conversations. We would be a little loose in that apartment."

It was important to the mobsters that the elderly widow never leave the apartment unguarded, because that meant the FBI could not get in to plant a bug. They could be "loose" there. But, to be completely accurate, Gravano should have said, "*nearly* always home," and the "nearly" made all the difference: the widow went to visit family—relatives, that is—for Thanksgiving. That was all the opening the FBI needed. The United States Attorney's Office for the Eastern District of New York went to a federal judge in Manhattan, who authorized the placement of a listening device in the apartment.

Late on Thanksgiving night, agents with a court order quietly entered the building and crept into the widow's tiny apartment, made up of two rooms connected by a small kitchen. Reasoning that the Gambino leadership wouldn't sit on the old lady's brass bed, they focused on her small living room, with its two cream-colored armchairs facing a brown crescent couch across a glass coffee table. Her TV, cable box, and VCR sat on a stand beside one of the armchairs. This had to be the meeting spot. They put the bug in her VCR, borrowing some of its power supply to keep the device alive, reasoning that the mobsters were unlikely to watch old movies during their meetings and ruin the sound quality.

Gotti and Gravano used the apartment only five times during the life of the court order, but each conversation was devastating evidence. They got very loose. Gotti could be heard explaining an order he had just issued for the murder of a family member who had failed to show appropriate respect to the boss: "You know why he is dying?" Gotti said. "He is gonna die because he refused to come in when I called. He didn't do nothing else wrong." Without revealing the bug, the FBI immediately warned the targeted mobster that colleagues might be planning to kill him. He was uninterested, and soon dead.

One January evening, Gotti, Gravano, and family consigliere—counselor—Frank Locascio gathered in the apartment to talk about the future of their crime family. The bug in the VCR captured the widow's stereo playing an instrumental version of Phil Collins's 1981 hit, "In the Air Tonight." Anyone who has ever drummed along on a steering wheel could imagine the "I've been waiting for this moment for all my life, oh Lord."

It was the right mood. They were about to induct—"make"—new Mafia members, and Gotti lamented the narrowness of those they were inducting into the family. "I want guys that done more than just killin'," he said. But pickings were slim and there were few "good" kids, those fully committed to a life of crime:

> And where are we gonna find them, these kinda guys? Frank, I'm not being a, a pessimist. It's gettin' tougher, not easier! We got everything that's any good. . . . I told you a couple weeks ago we got the only few pockets of good kids left. Look at this fuckin' bum. Your father's a cop, the uncle's a cop, the mother's a pain in the ass.

With that depressing prologue, they reviewed the list they were required to circulate to the other four New York Mafia families declaring their new Gambino members. This was a problem.

They didn't know the given names of their new soldiers. During the conversation, they struggled to recall the real names of colleagues like "Tommy from New Jersey" and "Fat Dom." With that problem solved, they turned to the challenge of reusing the names of dead members. From 1957 to 1975, the American Mafia did not make any new members. In 1957, La Cosa Nostra "closed the books" because of serious concerns about quality control. After eighteen years, they finally agreed each family could make ten new members. Gravano and John Gambino, a distant cousin of the family namesake, had been among that all-star gangster class for their family in 1975. (Gotti didn't get in that year because he was in jail.) But after 1975, the families agreed, new members were permitted to replace only those who died. New guys needed to be matched with the names of dead guys on a list shared among the families. Of course, this being the Mafia, families cheated and periodically reused the names of dead guys. But care was required to avoid using the same dead guy two years in a row. The bug captured the Gambino family leadership reviewing the dead and the living to make sure they wouldn't get caught.

After sorting all this out, and amending their list, the leaders realized their work now looked sloppy. The given names were in different handwriting from the nicknames, which was embarrassing. They agreed to rewrite the list in a single hand, and in four additional originals to pass to the other families.

Despite all the headaches, Gotti—like so many mobsters—believed he was part of something lasting and important. "This is gonna be a Cosa Nostra till I die," he assured his leadership team. "Be it an hour from now, or be it tonight, or a hundred years from now, when I'm in jail. It's gonna be a Cosa Nostra."

This was all true. His words would be around a hundred years from now. And he would die in jail. There was a bug in the VCR.

When I became FBI director years later, I obtained a copy of the October 1963 memo from J. Edgar Hoover to Attorney General Robert F. Kennedy seeking permission to conduct electronic surveillance of Dr. Martin Luther King Jr. At the bottom of the single-page memo, which is only five sentences long and without meaningful facts, Kennedy's signature grants that authority, without limit as to time or place. I put the memo under the glass on the corner of my FBI desk.

I kept the Hoover memo there not to make a critical statement about Kennedy or Hoover—despite there being lots to criticize—but to make a statement about the value of oversight and constraint. Hoover no doubt believed his cause was just, and Kennedy was afraid not to go along with Hoover. Among the problems with that dynamic was that they lacked meaningful testing of their assumptions. There was nothing to check them. I would explain to FBI employees who asked about the memo that to change the future we had to stare at the past, no matter how much it hurt. Especially when it came to our power to conduct electronic surveillance—when so much of life and privacy is electronic, we need to be constrained, overseen, and checked, lest we fall in love with our own righteousness and abuse our power. The importance of that oversight was drilled into me as a young prosecutor. Years later, as FBI director, I would see its value even more clearly in the world of national security wiretaps, where the stakes are higher and the shadows deeper. But that more complicated future was decades off.

A criminal wiretap application is drafted by the federal prosecutor assigned to the investigation, who will end up using evidence from the wiretap in a prosecution, and the case agent, who is the prosecutor's partner throughout. They create the application together, checking and arguing and drafting. Once they have obtained the necessary internal Department of Justice approvals—which is a rigorous process but involves fewer reviews than a national security wiretap—the prosecutor and agent will go see a federal judge, raise their right hands before that judge, and ask her to approve the surveillance. If she does, they will listen to their targets or read their emails and texts, then attempt to use what they get as evidence in a criminal case, but not before defense lawyers get the chance to see what they told the judge to get the court order and then attack it in open court.

I remember being told as a young prosecutor that there is a strong "pucker factor" in criminal wiretaps, for both agent and prosecutor, because their asses will be on the line for every word of the application. I have raised my right hand and felt the squeeze, but the payoff from doing it right can be extraordinary.

In the cold November of my third year as a federal prosecutor, just before my twenty-ninth birthday, we got permission to listen to the jewelry-district mobsters' office phone and to the boss's home phone. The case agent and I went to a federal judge's chambers, where the judge went through every page of a long application and then made both of us swear it was all true, accurate, and complete. We were both on the line now, but it was worth it. Almost immediately, the agents couldn't believe their ears: the mobsters appeared to be commissioning robbers to go steal for them and planning their own robberies, including of a large jewelry store. It was too good to be true; so good that we ended up having to stop them.

The phone calls about the jewelry-store-robbery plan were unclear about the location and the participants. But something big was going on, no doubt about it. The boss kept talking about it on the phone as he recruited participants. He told one, "I'll be fuckin' right outside.

I'll be supervising the whole thing. Now, my friend works in there. You understand. So it's a setup. Ya put the fuckin' gate down, ya take the showcases, the fuckin' vault, and leave." It would be a daylight armed robbery with a big crew of robbers and many innocent employees. Where or when, we didn't know, but it was coming soon. And we knew only a few of the players. Although the FBI didn't have enough evidence to make any arrests, we couldn't sit by and let a major daylight armed robbery happen someplace in New York. And it was too risky to try to follow possible participants and arrest them as they entered the jewelry store, guns drawn. Innocent people might get hurt that way, and, besides, only on TV is it possible to follow people in a major city without losing them.

How are we going to stop a major crime without blowing the wiretap? We can't just tell them "we have a tap on the boss's phone, so we are onto you." That would waste years of work to get to a court-ordered wiretap. But we also can't let a big armed robbery happen. There was no playbook for this. The agents came up with a good plan, which life turned into a genius plan. Although it would likely end our chance to prosecute, they planned to disrupt the robbery by confronting the most junior member of the conspiracy, a twenty-year-old the gangsters called "the kid." From the intercepted calls, it seemed the kid worked at the target jewelry store. He was the "friend [who] works in there." The agents would tell him somebody had ratted him out and the FBI knew all about the conspiracy. Maybe the bluff would flip the kid and he would give it up, but, worst case, it would stop the robbery. And the FBI would deploy surveillance teams in case the kid did something stupid that helped us figure out more about the scheme. Maybe, just maybe, it would "tickle the wire" by generating conversation where we could listen.

As planned, agents knocked on the door and told the kid the FBI knew all about the robbery scheme. Somebody had ratted him out.

He should cooperate to save himself, while there was still time. The kid was clearly rattled that the FBI knew he was at his sister's house (the surveillance team followed him there). As the leader of the group later told another participant on the wiretapped phone, "And this fuckin' kid did a fuckin' shit, ya know, half a fuckin' trembler." The agents did see his hands visibly shake, but he said he knew nothing and didn't want to talk to them. They left.

As the hidden FBI surveillance teams watched, the kid did something stupid. He quickly left the house, went to a public, coin-operated pay phone—relics today, but in the late 1980s a feature of many New York City street corners—and within minutes was with the next most senior member of the gang. Those two then went to a pay phone and called their boss at home. It was a lucky break for us—we had the court-ordered wiretap on the boss's home phone—but likely to be short-lived because the men at the pay phone did the smart thing. They opened the call by telling the boss, "We got trouble. I want you to go out to a pay phone and call me back, I'm on a pay phone." Smart move. Unfortunately, the FBI was only going to hear a few seconds of this call. It was impossible to quickly get a court order to listen in on some pay phone in Brooklyn, even if we knew what phone they would use.

But the boss didn't want to go to a pay phone. He would have to drive, because there were no nearby pay phones in the Long Island suburbs, where he lived. His wife had his car. Cell phones hadn't been invented yet. They begged him. Please, please go to a pay phone. Nah, he wasn't gonna do it. He assured them that they could speak safely on his home phone: "My phone's all right man," he said, but still the junior gangsters resisted.

"Just talk vague, man," the boss directed.

"No, I can't. I gotta tell you the whole story, man. This is serious," one replied.

"How serious?"

"Very serious. You think I'd be tellin' you this if it wasn't serious?"

When the boss still wouldn't go to a secure phone, the gangsters tried vague: "They know fuckin' a lot of things."

"Unless they have proof they can go fuck themselves," the boss replied.

He was not going to go to a pay phone, so they started talking, gingerly at first. The boss referred to a conspirator only by the code name "Mr. B," speculating that law enforcement must have discovered the plot because "his fuckin', his, his, his phone must be bugged, uh, Mr. B's." When the underling said that he didn't know Mr. B's last name, the boss hesitated. He then whispered it on the phone. In a clear whisper, he said the name—Facciolo. I know because we taped it. Didn't even need to turn up the volume to make out the name. Very clear whisperer, this guy. And the whisper had consequences. It allowed us to later arrest Mr. B—Lucchese crime family made member Bruno Facciolo—and one of his top associates, Larry Taylor. Facciolo, as was required under Mafia rules, had given his permission for the robbery to take place on his turf, and would get a piece of the loot as tribute. The arrests had unintended consequences for them. They were both murdered by the Mob shortly after they made bail. Mr. B was found in the trunk of a car with a dead canary jammed in his mouth. The Mafia worried he was going to cooperate with law enforcement. Taylor was later killed because the Mafia feared he might get emotional about Bruno's death and retaliate.

The boss later called another robbery conspirator—using the same wiretapped home phone—to warn him of the FBI's involvement, and followed his own advice to talk vague, telling his fellow criminal that the "F-E-Ds" were onto them.

Having spelled and whispered on the phone, as though the threat came from a toddler in the back seat, the callers slowly relaxed and tried to puzzle through who the "rat" was, a process that required them to review, in multiple phone calls, the name and loyalty of each member of the conspiracy, all on a wiretapped phone. At the end, they were certain there was no rat and the FBI must have been bluffing. For our part, we were now certain of everyone involved and had enough evidence to prosecute them. A win-win, really.

In 1991, a Manhattan federal jury got the chance to listen to the conversations at a trial of some of the robbers. The jurors sat in the jury box, wearing large headphones and looking down at a written transcript. They listened as one begged the other to go to a pay phone and received the instruction to "talk vague." When the calls got to the whispering and spelling, nearly the entire jury looked up and laughed. The F-E-Ds indeed.

After three years of work, I indicted sixteen defendants. Seven of them went to trial together in Manhattan. The wiretap recordings—the product of months of meticulous work overseen by a federal judge—were damning evidence, and I interspersed them among dozens of witnesses during the two-month trial. Then I stood, buttoned my jacket, and told the court, "The government rests," meaning we had finished putting on our case. It was the defendants' turn.

Only one of the seven defendants had no criminal record, so he was apparently nominated to explain it all away. "Joey Diamonds," as he was known, took the witness stand and told the jury he had once considered becoming a lawyer but buying and selling entirely legitimate precious stones had become his passion; hence the nickname. He then spent most of a day telling a complicated story of how the witnesses were liars and the wiretap conversations were all actually about a legitimate plan to borrow jewelry on consignment from a large jewelry store. The FBI had completely misunderstood. The urgent codes in their conversations were a product of their concern that a sensitive, but entirely legal, transaction had gone awry and would harm important commercial relationships. They were businesspeople, worried that the FBI was under a serious misapprehension, a fear that regrettably came true when they were all indicted for racketeering. It was understandable that the government was confused, but a tragedy nonetheless.

It was preposterous. I was going to crush this guy on cross-examination. But as I watched him finish his fifth hour smoothly lying in response to his own lawyer's questions and then those of his co-defendants, I got angry. It was all some kind of game to them. Everyone in the courtroom knew he was lying, including the defense lawyers. The oath meant nothing. It was all one big wink. He was just doing what had to be done. Har har.

When the judge called on me, I approached the podium with my notebook open, the cross-examination plan sketched out. I looked down at my first question and paused. Something snapped. I did the only intentionally improper thing I have ever done in a courtroom.

THE COURT: Mr. Comey, you may proceed with your cross-examination.

MR. COMEY: Thank you, Your Honor. Sir, I'm not going to hold you to a number, but can you give me some idea of how many hours it took you to think up this story you just told on direct examination?

DEFENSE COUNSEL: Objection.

THE COURT: Objection sustained.

The judge looked pained by what I had done, betrayed even. The question was sarcastic, argumentative, and abusive in form. I immediately felt guilty. "I'll move on," I said, and began the cross I had planned.

When the trial ended, we decided it made sense for agents to interview the alternate jurors, who had not deliberated, to see if we could improve our case because we still had defendants to try. One of the agents—the committed bachelor who had also made the fake fur robbery case—quickly volunteered to interview Alternate #1, an attractive woman who had said during the selection process that she was single. He called her home phone and was leaving a message when she apparently decided not to screen him. She picked up the phone and in a warm Southern accent said she would be happy to meet him, adding, "The least you people could do is buy me a beer." The interview was productive, and the New York agent who avoided long relationships entered one, marrying former Alternate Juror #1, the love of his life, and starting a family.

Long after the trial, she thanked me for my improper question. Former Alternate Juror #1 said the jury felt the same growing unease blossoming into anger as they sat stone-faced watching Joey Diamonds lie for five hours. At the first break after my inappropriate question, they filed into the jury room and burst into smiles and laughter, high-fiving each other over my improper question. "I'm glad you enjoyed it," I said, "but I still shouldn't have done it."

I wasn't just being polite. I shouldn't have done it. At the age of thirty, I spent eight weeks in that courtroom representing the United States in a good way, insisting that my deeply flawed witnesses tell the truth, reveal their bad acts, and behave with dignity. And then I stood up and asked a question I knew was wrong. It was unacceptable. I let my emotions cloud my judgment, and by doing something improper I risked not only my own reputation, but something more important—the reservoir of trust that attracted me to the work in the first place. I was too immature to realize I was risking something priceless.

CHAPTER 6

THE NICE PART OF AMERICA

If you do not tell the truth about yourself you cannot
tell it about other people.
Virginia Woolf

SOMEBODY HAD TO SIT ON THE BED, which was awkward. Marriott's Courtyards and Hilton's Gardens just hadn't imagined two prosecutors, one FBI agent, and a hidden mobster in the same room, for an entire day. The United States Marshals Service, which ran the Witness Security Program (also often called the Witness Protection Program), wasn't going to spring for a conference room; that would cost too much and draw too much attention. At neutral-site visits, somebody had to sit on the bed, maybe all day.

Prosecutors and agents were not permitted to know where in America the government had hidden our witnesses. WitSec, or "the program," was tightly compartmented, which was why no protected witness who followed the rules had ever been killed. If the witness followed the rules—if we all followed the rules—they would stay safe. That, a mobster once explained to me, was the government's real power over organized crime—the ability to deliver safety to those who betrayed La Cosa Nostra. Gambino family underboss Salvatore "Sammy the Bull" Gravano told me that he and family boss John Gotti would fantasize about killing someone in the program. It didn't matter who, he explained. They just needed to get to somebody, anybody, and the government would lose power. If a potential witness, or his family, nursed any doubt about the program, the Mob won.

America's size and mobility helped. The Italians didn't have that advantage. A Sicilian mobster who decided to become a government witness—a *pentiti*—had few places to hide. No place on the island of Sicily would be safe. And a Sicilian would stick out like a sore thumb in Tuscany or the remote villages of the Dolomites. But in America, strange names or odd accents were everywhere. As a Manhattan prosecutor, I joked that there were two Americas: the part that generated Mafia witnesses in need of relocation, and the nice part, where we hid them.

We never knew where they were hidden. Sure, we picked up clues, like when a Brooklyn mobster mentioned his newfound affection for the Kansas City Chiefs football team, but once we applied to the Department of Justice for them to disappear, the Marshals Service took it from there. To see our disappeared witness again, we asked the Marshals to arrange a "neutral site," offering a range of possible dates, but no places. The Marshals chose the places. We would be told to stay at a particular hotel in a particular city on a particular day. It wasn't where the witness lived. It was a neutral site. From wherever he lived, the Marshals would bring the witness, but not to our hotel. The witness would stay somewhere else. And we wouldn't meet at our hotel, or wherever the witness was staying. Instead, on the day of the meeting, we would be given a room number at a third hotel, where our witness and his Marshals handler awaited us, probably already in the room's only chairs.

There must have been some logic to the neutral site selection process, but I never figured it out. Sometimes they sent me to lovely, warm places, sometimes not. I met Vincent DiMarco in late December in Sioux Falls, South Dakota. The lunchtime temperature peaked at two degrees Fahrenheit and steadily dropped from there. It was clear from our clothing and our poor attitudes that neither of us lived in the northern plains. I felt badly for him. Life had been hard, even for a mobbed-up drug dealer.

Vinnie had been a caterer, running a popular suburban New York spot for wedding receptions, when his son Bennie failed at being a drug dealer, and in a dangerous way. Bennie took money up front—a lot of money—from some Brooklyn mobsters and failed to deliver the drugs. He failed because he was an addict and got ripped off by some South Florida drug dealers, but he still failed, in a way that could cost his life. To save him, Vinnie became a drug dealer, promising the Brooklyn mobsters he would take over for his son and make them whole. Vinnie became a criminal, but he had to; his two sons were his life. He couldn't bear to lose another one.

Five years earlier, three sons were his life. The oldest, Vincent Junior, was his pride and joy. Five years before Vinnie became a drug dealer, Vincent Junior and Bennie had a terrible fight at the DiMarco home. During their altercation, Bennie produced a gun. Vincent Junior grabbed for it. They struggled, four hands on the gun, rolling on the floor. The gun went off. Bennie stopped moving. Blood seeped from under his still body. In the silence of the DiMarco home, Vincent Junior realized he had killed his brother. He pulled the gun from under Bennie, pressed it to his own head, and pulled the trigger. His lifeless body fell next to Bennie's.

But Bennie was alive. A New York City ambulance took him to the hospital, where he recovered from the gunshot wound. Vincent Senior did not recover. Several months later, he checked himself into a hotel room and tried to commit suicide with pills. He failed, and was hospitalized. He tried again, and failed. He was committed to a psychiatric facility. After a long road of treatment, Vinnie returned to catering. Until Bennie failed at being a drug dealer.

Vinnie was also a poor drug dealer. His first heroin customer, as he tried to earn back what his son owed some very bad people, turned out to be an undercover DEA agent. The DEA arrested Vinnie, and threatened to arrest Bennie if Vinnie didn't become an informant. He agreed. Although Vinnie had been a failure as a dealer, it turned out he was pretty good at pretending to be a successful dealer, using the DEA's money to restore his relationships with the Mob. So Vinnie spent two years being an informant, meeting with Mafia drug dealers and turning the drugs he bought over to the DEA. Then the feds arrested brothers John and Joe Gambino and members of their drug dealing crew and Vinnie disappeared into America. But he disappeared alone, because his family disowned him after learning he wasn't a real drug dealer. His wife said she didn't want to be married to a rat. Vinnie went alone.

Of course, he didn't go as Vinnie, but by some other name that I never knew. As always, the program put him someplace where nobody knew him. As always, the Marshals expected him to earn a legitimate living using whatever lawful skills and education he had. This was a constant problem with relocated mobsters who had dropped out of school to bully people after the eighth grade. With killing, robbing, and extorting off the table, options for legitimate work were limited. But Vinnie was a skilled restaurateur. Using his new identity, he borrowed money and opened an Italian place. He splurged on the neon sign over the entrance. In big, bright letters, it announced that this place was VINNIE's.

At Vinnie's invitation, his handler from the Marshals Service stopped by for the grand opening. The deputy marshal glanced up at the big sign.

"That's gotta go."

"Wha? The sign? It's not my name anymore."

"Vinnie," the marshal replied, "anybody walks in here with any connection to your old life, looks at you, looks at the sign, they're gonna put it together. Get rid of the sign."

Vinnie changed the sign. I never knew the new name, but the business did well. People in the nice part of America love good Italian food.

Vinnie and I got the chairs in Sioux Falls. The FBI special agent sat on the bed. Vinnie seemed fragile, his cracked voice difficult to hear over the heating unit under the window. My job was to figure out whether he was able to testify. Could he recall his DEA-supervised deals with the Gambino crew we were prosecuting? Could he keep it together on the witness stand in a cavernous Manhattan federal courtroom, staring at mobsters? I tried to build rapport, to show empathy. How was he doing? How was he feeling? Much better, he reported. Still taking Prozac, but no memory-loss problems, no thoughts of suicide. His life had stabilized. "I fell in love with a wonderful woman at my new place. She doesn't know anything about my old life, but she doesn't need to. She married me because she loves me. And I love her. We are really happy."

Although I was tempted to ask about the sustainability of a relationship based on not knowing your new spouse is a relocated drug dealer the Mob wants to kill, a more immediate question came out of me:

"Did you say you got *married*?"

Vinnie nodded. "Civil ceremony."

"Vinnie, you are already married." His wife might have disowned him, but they had never divorced.

"That was Vincent DiMarco. I'm another person now."

"In a sense," I answered, "but you are the same human being,

Vinnie, and you can't be married to two people at the same time. It's against the law. Called bigamy."

"Well, I am, and I love her, and she loves me."

"I don't doubt that, and I'm very happy for you."

I dropped the bigamy, for now. This get-together in freezing Sioux Falls was about empathy and rapport. But bigamy wasn't going away.

I didn't know where Vinnie lived, but I knew it was a crime in all fifty states to be married twice, simultaneously. There are nineteen states where you can marry your cousin but there is no place where you can be married to *two* of your cousins at the same time. We weren't going to turn Vinnie in for his bigamy, so in a sense we were giving him immunity. He had also promised he would not commit any crimes; his new marriage broke that promise.

The Department of Justice has an obligation to tell defendants and their lawyers bad stuff about the government's witnesses. For a trial to be fair, defense lawyers must have any information they can use to undercut—"impeach" is the word courts use—the credibility of government witnesses. The requirement comes from the due process clause of the Fifth Amendment to the United States Constitution. Given the government's power, a trial would not be fair—it would not be "due process"—if prosecutors didn't share facts that undercut a witness's credibility, such as prior criminal records or other acts of misconduct of the government witness, promises of leniency or immunity. The obligation only runs one way; defense lawyers don't need to share bad stuff they know about their witnesses. That makes sense, given the power of the government. The Department of Justice has the ability to accuse people of crimes and lock them up. For that reason, prosecutors bear the burden of proving guilt, the defendant has the right to remain silent, and only one side has to show its dirty laundry.

The bigamy was dirty laundry. To meet our obligations as Department of Justice lawyers, we had to give the lawyers for the Gambino brothers this information.

Vinnie freaked out. Shortly before his testimony, I met with him in a New York–area safe house run by the Marshals. I told him I needed to disclose his double marriage. His color changed and his chin dropped to his chest. I also told him the Marshals Service was going to connect him with a trusted private lawyer who would immediately begin the process of obtaining a divorce from his wife in New York. The divorce had to be under way before he testified. He wouldn't lift his head, wouldn't speak to me. It was bad enough that I was bringing him back to New York to face a courtroom of fearsome mobsters. I was forcing him to talk about a life of ruin and pain, of unspeakable loss. On top of all that, I was now requiring him to speak publicly about the relationship that had steadied him in his new life. And speak about that relationship like it was a crime. He just didn't get it. I suppressed, "Well, it *is* a crime, Vinnie, in all fifty states, including places where you can marry your close relatives." This was about letting him adjust to what was nonnegotiable. He had committed a crime. Very few people knew about it, and the jury surely wouldn't care, but that didn't matter. We had obligations that were nonnegotiable: we knew something that could be used to impeach him and we needed to make sure lawyers for the Gambino crime family knew.

I explained to Vinnie that I was simply going to ask him about it during his testimony. That way, the defense lawyers would know. If they wanted to ask him about it, they could. And he could explain, just as he had to me in frigid Sioux Falls, that he didn't think of it as a crime, that this new love was his rock, after so much dysfunction, crime, and loss. And so, in front of the jury, I asked:

"When you went in the Witness Protection Program four years ago, did your family go with you?"

"No, I was all by myself."

"Were you married at the time?"

"Yes. I lost everything."

"Your wife did not go with you?"

"No, no."

"While you've been in the Witness Protection Program have you married another woman?"

"Yes."

"And you have not yet divorced your wife who left you when you went in the program?"

"Right, we're working on that now."

On cross-examination, Joe Gambino's lawyer hit the bigamy. He dropped it as quickly as he touched it. Because Vinnie was resigned to it, even beaten by it:

"So you're not divorced yet; is that right?"

When Vinnie agreed, the lawyer added, "So you're living this sham with a woman that you're presently with; is that right?"

"That's right, sir," Vinnie exhaled.

A sham. His love was now a sham. The defense lawyer moved on. I felt sorry for Vinnie in that moment. But the truth was more important than his pain, something other cooperating witnesses would discover. No matter how much it hurt, the Department of Justice could not accept anything short of the whole truth and nothing but the truth. If the government didn't honor that obligation, the system could not be just.

CHAPTER 7

MEN OF HONOR

I'm for truth, no matter who tells it.
MALCOLM X

THE WEDDING PROCESSION WOUND ITS WAY through the whitewashed Sicilian village. It was a joyous and important occasion. Mafia member Pietro Vernengo's daughter, Rosa, was marrying a rising star in the Sicilian Cosa Nostra, twenty-eight-year-old Francesco Marino Mannoia. The marriage had been arranged by the family—the crime family—and Mannoia embraced it because it was good for his career. The tall, thin, cerebral Mannoia, his light brown hair tracing a widow's peak, was quite the catch for the Vernengo family—the relatives. Although he had dropped out of school in the eighth grade to pursue a life of crime, he was very good at it. He had stolen for the Mafia, smuggled for the Mafia, and made himself extraordinarily valuable to both the Sicilian and American Mafias by learning to refine morphine delivered by Turkish traffickers into snow-white Sicilian heroin. His work generated millions of dollars in heroin trade on both sides of the Atlantic.

Shortly after becoming engaged to Rosa, he was formally "combined" into Cosa Nostra, becoming an official member, a *uomo d'onore*—man of honor. Mannoia was so valuable that families competed for him, and he joined Cosa Nostra as a member not of the Brancaccio family, into whose territory he had been born, but into the Santa Maria di Gesú family, led by the fearsome Stefano Bontate, who not only led Santa Maria di Gesú—its *representate*—but sat on the Commission that ruled over all of Sicilian Cosa Nostra. Bontate explained to Mannoia during his induction ceremony that Cosa Nostra hated the word "Mafia," which they viewed as a literary creation. He was never to use it again. He was now part of Cosa Nostra—"this thing of ours." He would obey its laws and customs and die part of Cosa Nostra, which was the only way out. And Bontate explained that Mannoia would not be assigned to a *capodecima*—a boss of ten—as other *soldati* were; he was to report directly and exclusively to Bontate. He was a star.

But there was a problem, which was standing along the marriage parade route, tears streaming down her face and dripping off her chin onto her pregnant belly. After his engagement to Rosa Vernengo, Mannoia had fallen in love with Rita Simoncini, a woman with no connections to Cosa Nostra, and she was pregnant with their first child. Rita was fun and smart and passionate and alive. He loved her in a way he would never love Rosa. Before the wedding, Mannoia told Rosa the truth—that he was in love with another woman, who was pregnant with his child. He told her he was sorry, but he didn't love her. She was disappointed, but they both knew there was no turning back. Mannoia could not ask to be relieved from a Cosa Nostra engagement. He was a man of honor who had promised another man of honor he would marry his daughter. Her brothers were also Cosa Nostra soldiers. This match was a big deal in the family. It was business and tradition. A priest blessed the union and they marched.

He didn't turn his head as they passed Rita. He couldn't, not without making his wife a widow and his unborn daughter fatherless.

But having pledged in separate ceremonies that he would be true to his wife and never lie to another man of honor, Mannoia planned carefully to betray both of those oaths.

In a federal courtroom in Manhattan in 1993, facing American mobster John Gambino, the recipient of so much of his pure white heroin, Mannoia explained what he had done:

"Why didn't you ever break off the engagement with Rosa Vernengo?"

"I had become a man of honor, and besides being a man of honor, in Sicily there is a very special custom—by custom I mean way of living, way of thinking mostly. In order to break an engagement in Sicily there have to be very serious reasons for that to happen. One cannot say to his relatives, to his family, and to the people who live around him that one breaks that engagement because he has fallen in love with another woman."

"Did you marry Rosa Vernengo?"

"Yes."

"Is divorce allowed in Cosa Nostra in Sicily?"

"No."

"Did you continue to see Rita Simoncini after you married Rosa Vernengo?"

"Yes."

Mannoia maintained two households, commuting between Rosa and Rita and their daughter. It worked for five years, then took a dangerous turn, when he suspected rivals were going to tell his boss. So he did it first.

"Did you ever discuss that relationship with your boss in Cosa Nostra, Stefano Bontate?"

"Yes, once."

"What was said?"

". . . I went to see my *representate,* Stefano Bontate, and I told him about my situation before the other people would tell him. Stefano Bontate told me that I had to leave that woman, meaning Rita Simoncini, even though she was the mother of my daughter, because I was a married man and because I also was a man of honor. He told me that I had to take complete care of my daughter, but that I had to stop seeing Rita Simoncini."

"What did you say?"

"I lied to my boss, because I said yes to him. I lied for love."

"Did you continue to see the woman after you told him you wouldn't?"

"Yes. That's why I lied to him. . . . For love I was jeopardizing my life."

Bontate was murdered two years after Mannoia lied to him, shot by multiple assailants with AK-47s as he crossed the sidewalk from his own mistress's house to his bulletproof car. A horrific war over the heroin trade was ripping through Cosa Nostra. Hundreds of men of honor were murdered, all over the world. Mannoia was spared because he was in jail, but also because his skills as a chemist in the drug trade were so valuable. A new boss, aligned with the victorious, real-life Corleone family—a name immortalized in *The Godfather*—came to see him in jail, to assess his loyalty. The new boss asked about Rita. Mannoia lied again for love. He then escaped from jail and began refining morphine into heroin for the Corleonesi.

Five years later, Mannoia was back in jail after being recaptured by Italian police when he started to get a bad feeling. His brother, another man of honor, disappeared, leaving behind only his car and his blood soaked into the driver's seat. Mannoia decided that the only way to see his daughter grow up was to betray Cosa Nostra, to become a government witness—what the Italians called a *pentiti*. The Italian government appeared to finally have honest, competent prosecutors pursuing Cosa Nostra. Maybe they could help him leave in an unusual way—alive. So he quietly reached out to one of the prosecutors and had a single meeting with him. Within weeks, Cosa Nostra sent a horrific message. Mannoia's mother, sister, aunt, uncle, and cousin were brutally murdered.

It had the opposite of the intended effect.

"Sometimes I am afraid," Mannoia said, staring at us with sad eyes ringed in dark circles. He exhaled a cloud of smoke at me, Patrick Fitzgerald—my co-prosecutor on the case—and an FBI special agent. The Marshals had found us a neutral-site hotel room where he could smoke. The United States government had brought him—with Rita and their daughter and without Rosa Vernengo, who stayed in Sicily—to America and hidden them in one of the nice places. Now we needed him to testify about all that heroin he refined for Cosa Nostra to ship to John Gambino, the man who connected the two Mafia worlds.

"But when I grow afraid, I remember what they did to me. I carry with me always an image that reminds me of why I must destroy Cosa Nostra. It gives me strength when I am afraid." It was a powerful metaphor, the mental image of the horrific price he had paid for betraying the Mafia. I could imagine how it stayed with him. But then he leaned forward, hinged his arm back and began digging in his rear pants pocket. He pulled out his bifold wallet, spread the bill compartment, and retrieved a folded piece of newspaper. With his lit cigarette pinched between two fingers of his left hand, he began unfolding the paper and smoothing it on the little hotel coffee table with the palms of his hands, rotating it so we could see the image. It was from an Italian newspaper. In black and white, the bullet-riddled bodies of two late-middle-aged women and a young woman were shown slumped over in a car. It was his mother, his aunt, and his sister. "It gives me strength." We took a break.

Mannoia was to be a devastating witness for the United States

Department of Justice in the prosecution of John Gambino. With his extraordinary memory, Mannoia could recount for an American jury how the Sicilian-born, Brooklyn-bred Gambino became the channel—*il canale*—between the two Cosa Nostra worlds. Mannoia had personally refined huge amounts of heroin for shipment to Gambino. He saw this important man visit the Sicilian countryside to inspect the brutal refining process, during which Mannoia worked twenty-four-hour shifts, watching his skin bleach and peel off. At Gambino's request, Mannoia changed his methods, so that a plant-based dilutant called tropine was not blended with heroin during production, but shipped separately so the American mobsters could decide their own purity levels for America's addicts.

Mannoia knew what Gambino and Stefano Bontate—Mannoia's boss or *representate*—did with the huge profits from the heroin trade, turning millions over to prominent Italian American banker Michele Sindona to launder and invest. The flamboyant Sicilian-born Sindona operated in both countries and described himself to the media as "a bridge between American industry and European industry because I know both." Sindona was a financial adviser to the Vatican and Pope Paul VI, and to leaders of the Sicilian and American Mafias. He knew many secrets. But so did Mannoia.

Mannoia knew what happened when Sindona's banking empire collapsed with the failure of his American crown jewel, New York–based Franklin National Bank. The largest bank failure in American history was quickly followed by allegations of fraud on both sides of the Atlantic. Sindona was arrested and set to go on trial in Manhattan federal court, a prospect that made Cosa Nostra very nervous. They didn't care about the Franklin National Bank or its shareholders and depositors. They cared about Sindona. They needed time with him, in private, to learn where he had put their money and enlist his help to retrieve it, before he disappeared into the American federal prison system.

Mannoia knew the secret of what they did. It was extraordinarily risky, but then there was a lot of money at stake. John Gambino arranged to have Sindona "kidnapped" off the street in Manhattan on the eve of his federal bank fraud trial. The "kidnappers" then sent bizarre political ransom demands to government offices in America and Italy. But the people who bundled Sindona into a waiting car weren't Italian revolutionaries. He wasn't tied up in some basement apartment on the American East Coast and moved constantly among safe houses. He was long gone. There were no leftist kidnappers; there was only Cosa Nostra.

Gambino supplied false identity papers and a disguise to fly Sindona to Greece, where he was ferried by boat across the Ionian Sea to Sicily. As the New York police looked for radical kidnappers, Sindona ate, slept, and answered Cosa Nostra questions in a mountain villa outside Palermo. Sindona was too important to kill at the moment, so Gambino and Bontate planned how they would end the charade. Early in Sindona's eight-week stay, an Italian American doctor visited the villa. Sindona removed his pants and the doctor injected a painkiller into Sindona's right thigh. As Gambino held Sindona's shoulders to keep him still, Bontate shot the banker through the thigh using a small-caliber handgun. The doctor supervised his recovery.

After eight weeks away, Sindona was taken from the Sicilian villa to Frankfurt, Germany, where he flew to New York. His "kidnappers" pushed him out of a car onto a Manhattan street. Sindona was free, and told his harrowing tale, including his brave attempt to escape from the revolutionaries somewhere in New England, during which he was shot.

Sindona's trial went forward. He was convicted of bank fraud and sentenced to twenty-five years in American prison. The United States Department of Justice transported him to Italy so he could stand trial there for fraud and the contract murder of the Italian lawyer appointed to serve as trustee and unwind Sindona's complicated Italian financial empire. Four days after his conviction for hiring the trustee's killer, Sindona was murdered in his Italian jail cell by cyanide-laced coffee. The banker for Cosa Nostra and the Vatican wasn't needed any longer. He would be silent forever.

Mannoia not only knew what really happened but he could explain a tantalizing clue about John Gambino's role. Just about the time Sindona was returning to the United States so he could be "released" in Manhattan by his kidnappers, Italian cops stopped Gambino as he was departing his hotel—bags packed—in Palermo, Sicily. They held him only long enough to ask him to empty his pockets. In a nice piece of police work, they photocopied a small slip of paper that meant nothing to them; on it was written, "741 sabato francoforte." Long after, the FBI learned about the paper in Gambino's pocket, asked the Italians for a copy, and went to work.

Gambino was stopped by the Italian police on a Friday, October 12. The FBI quickly discovered that the next day, Saturday—*sabato*— October 13, TWA flight 741 departed Frankfurt—*francoforte*—for JFK. Agents went to the airport in New York and retrieved the box of customs declarations from flight 741. Wearing gloves, they carefully looked at every form submitted by adult males on the flight. One belonged to a Joseph Bonamico, who listed an address in Brooklyn, but misspelled his home borough as "Brooklin." Bonamico had also written the number 9 on the card by placing a small dot inside the 9, something the agents knew was a peculiar habit of Sindona's. They sent that card to the FBI lab, which found Sindona's fingerprint on it.

So Sindona had returned on flight 741, a reservation he made— as "Joseph Bonamico"—the day before his departure from Germany.

John Gambino, standing a thousand miles away, in the lobby of a Sicilian hotel, had flight information for Germany that was so recent that the ink on his slip of paper may have been wet. Mannoia could explain how that could be.

But we had a problem. We were in a hotel room in the nice part of America, and Mannoia had never killed anyone. In all his meetings with Italian investigators after becoming a *pentiti,* Mannoia had denied being involved in murder. He had been only a burglar, a robber, a forger, a heroin refiner, and a valuable member of Sicilian Cosa Nostra, an organization built on homicide, one where the induction ceremony involved dripping blood from the inductee's trigger finger onto the picture of a saint. He said his now-vanished brother had killed about three dozen people. But not him. When our predecessor prosecutors on the case asked him if he had killed anyone, he denied it, explaining that his unique role as a chemist allowed him to live without death.

My trial partner, Pat Fitzgerald, didn't believe it, and he wasn't going to use him as a witness if he didn't believe him. As lawyers for the Department of Justice, we couldn't.

The business of using the testimony of bad people to get more bad people is perilous work. It's essential—especially to take down sophisticated criminals, who don't surround themselves with upstanding future witnesses—but dangerous. A supervisor once warned me that every cooperating criminal witness "is a gun pointed at your career." But it was more than that. Because the government is responsible for ensuring that trials are fair, cooperating criminal witnesses—even though necessary to expose serious crimes—pose a mortal threat to the justice system. That was the reason our practice in the United States Attorney's Office for the Southern District of New York was to require cooperating witnesses to admit every crime they had ever committed.

All humans are complicated, but career criminals, who have spent their lives lying and manipulating just to survive, pose a special threat to the Department of Justice's obligation to find and tell the truth. If a prosecutor is being true to the core values of justice, these criminal witnesses' behavior couldn't be more in conflict with the way she has chosen to work. They have lived by angles, trying to find a way to cut a corner, or shade the truth; they have survived by bluff, bluster, and bullshit. For the Department of Justice lawyer, there can be no angles, no shade. In many ways, they are her opposite, yet she needs them to achieve a just result. But wherever they have been, she must insist they do things her way now. Easier said than done.

Mannoia's saying he had been in Sicilian Cosa Nostra for twenty-five years but never killed anyone was like saying you had spent a career in the NBA but never fouled anyone because your job was to make three-pointers.

But why would he lie? Mannoia had been loaned to us under a treaty that required immunity in America for any crime he had committed. And, in any event, he had never killed anyone in America, or even been here before. He had nothing to worry about from us. After we took over the case, Pat studied the record of all Mannoia's interactions with Italian authorities, looking for clues. He found one. In Mannoia's first conversations with Italian investigators, he revealed his involvement in hiding a weapon for another man of honor; the debriefings were halted and he was charged with that offense. It seemed that Italian law did not allow for immunity and prosecution was obligatory; his admissions required him to be charged. He then resumed his "secret" debriefings, which were next interrupted when Cosa Nostra murdered his mother, his sister, and his aunt. He never again admitted to anything new, including murder. And neither the Italians nor our predecessors as prosecutors on the case had ever really pressed him.

Fitzgerald pressed, hard. In emotional, hours-long conversations in hotel rooms throughout the country, Pat pushed Mannoia, telling him he didn't believe him. Nobody reported directly to Stefano Bontate who wasn't a killer. It just wasn't possible. And if it wasn't possible, he was lying. And if he was lying, he wasn't testifying. Our case against John Gambino depended upon Mannoia. It was tempting to let it slide rather than fail to bring a major American mobster to justice, but we were prepared to let the case collapse. And to make it harder, Fitzgerald told him he would be required to admit his crimes in open court in Manhattan, including that he had repeatedly lied about murders in Italian proceedings. The Italians would find out what he had done and he would have no protection against their prosecuting him for what he admitted in American court. Mannoia was angry and resisted.

Pat pushed, using honor and leverage. Despite the fact that he believed Mannoia had killed and knew him to be a massive heroin trafficker, Pat also knew his strange life was organized around his particular sense of honor. With a barely concealed sense of pride, Mannoia once told us the story of a Danish sailor who had been wrongly accused of slashing the face of an exotic dancer in a Palermo nightclub. Cosa Nostra *soldati* found the local Sicilian who had attacked the dancer, strangled him, and left his dead body on the steps of the police station, with a note pinned to his shirt: "I slashed the dancer." The police released the Dane, thanks to the "good" work of men of honor. In Mannoia's conception, he was a Cosa Nostra soldier who lived by a code, and lied only for love. Surely, Pat argued, Mannoia could see that in his new life as a soldier *against* Cosa Nostra, lying was also dishonorable. The American justice system was built around the truth, the whole truth, and nothing but the truth. Only people without honor lied under oath.

There was power in the honor pitch. Cosa Nostra members on both sides of the Atlantic really did imagine themselves as noble warriors. Maybe it was how they slept at night, dreaming they were people of principle who did difficult things in service to something larger than themselves. During the Gambino trial, the New York City Bar gave me the Stimson Medal, which recognizes outstanding federal prosecutors in the city. The award got minor mention in the newspaper. The next morning, as I walked into the courtroom, one of the deputy U.S. marshals who guarded our defendants—they were being held without bail during the trial—handed me a small, folded piece of paper. In my seat at the government's table, I unfolded the note. It was from one of our defendants, a young Mafia hit man once described by family boss John Gotti as "a real fucking man." That's why we were trying to put him in federal prison for the rest of his life.

He had good handwriting: "Dear Mr. Comey: Congratulations on the award. It is well deserved." I glanced back at him. He nodded solemnly. He wasn't being sarcastic; he wasn't trying to suck up or intimidate or send a secret message that he wanted to become a *pentiti*. It wasn't that complicated. He was a soldier. I was a soldier across the lines, a worthy opponent who conducted himself in an honorable way. Sure, I was trying to have him die in jail. But, in his view, it was nothing personal, just business. There was honor in it.

But we had more than honor with Mannoia. Our leverage was that lying would jeopardize what he loved most. We knew Mannoia wanted Rita and their young daughter to be safe in America, with him, in our famous Witness Security Program. If he wouldn't tell the truth, Pat explained, they would all go back to Italy. We had no wish to harm him, but if he wasn't our witness, he couldn't stay. And he couldn't stay if he didn't tell the truth. There were long silences, as Mannoia's sad eyes stared through the cigarette smoke. Mannoia started to break, telling Fitzgerald that if he answered the question about whether he had ever killed, Fitzgerald would surely follow up with "impertinent questions, as a wife, after her husband admits infidelity, demands to know how many times he cheated." He was ready to admit he was a murderer.

After speaking to his Italian lawyer, Mannoia agreed to a deal, which we put in writing so that, too, could be shown to the jury: Mannoia couldn't be prosecuted in America or Italy for any lies he had told to that point, but the Italians would be told whatever he admitted; his family would be safe in America; and if he lied again, the deal was off. It wasn't a great deal for us as prosecutors—defense lawyers would hammer him and us for forgiving perjury by one of our witnesses—but we were out of leverage. We would rather take that hit than let John Gambino go.

With the deal signed, the floodgates opened. Fitzgerald had been more right than he knew. Mannoia remembered participating in murdering twenty-five people. Victims were shot or strangled, a horrific process Mannoia described obsessively. Bodies were burned, buried, left to be found, or dissolved in acid. He remembered the names of the dead, but the particulars ran together in his mind. As he explained in court:

> Regrettably, on account of my dirty conscience that allows
> me to brag of nothing, as a matter of fact I've only things to
> be ashamed of and not to boast of, sometimes a person is able
> to remember one single fact because it is chiseled in his mind.
> If somebody killed somebody, he won't forget it his whole life
> through. He would even remember the most minute details.
> But when somebody has killed more than one man, the
> memory does not recall details.

Pat Fitzgerald could have avoided confronting Mannoia, pressuring him, appealing to his honor, risking our entire case. After all, Mannoia had already explained, under oath to Italian judges, that he was a specialist in Cosa Nostra, focused only on the technically difficult task of creating heroin from opium. As the chemist, he was far too valuable to be risked in acts of violence. The story would have flown. Maybe defense lawyers in the Gambino case would press him to admit murder, but maybe not; given the evidence of their own clients' membership in Cosa Nostra, why would they want to remind the jury that the organization was filled with homicidal maniacs? There was no reason to risk a break with Mannoia.

But it just didn't feel right to Fitzgerald. He had an obligation as a lawyer for the Department of Justice never to make an argument he didn't believe in. And he didn't believe Mannoia's "I was just a chemist" story. So he pressed and risked our case, for the truth. He got it and told it, exposing our key witness as a perjurer. He did it because he knew his client wasn't Mannoia or the United States Attorney in Manhattan; his client was an institution that had to be dedicated to the idea that truth was real and that it mattered above all else. So he told it, all of it.

CHAPTER 8

WAKING SAMMY

Truth never damages a cause that is just.
Mahatma Gandhi

SALVATORE "SAMMY THE BULL" Gravano was not a morning person. As we walked into the special federal prison for cooperating witnesses, the FBI agent from the squad that handled Gravano—the former number-two leader of the Gambino crime family, its underboss—explained to us that they tried never to visit Gravano before 10:00 A.M. because he liked to sleep late. Looking at his watch, he noted we were showing up just after nine; with a grimace, he said we shouldn't be surprised if the witness was in a bad mood.

The guy may have killed nineteen people and devoted his life to a savage criminal organization, but the United States government needed him. The boss of the Gambino family, John Gotti, had twice beaten indictments in New York, earning him the media nickname "Teflon Don." Gravano's guilty plea and cooperation meant the feds were finally going to get Gotti. That's why Gravano was allowed to plead guilty to a twenty-year cap—the sentencing judge could not give him more than twenty years in jail—and he was required to be a witness for only two years. It was an incredible deal for a serial killer and mob underboss, but the United States—through the U.S. Attorney in Brooklyn and the New York FBI—decided it needed his cooperation badly enough. And that power imbalance surrounded Gravano.

On our way to the jail, the escorting agent explained to me and Pat Fitzgerald that it would be important for us to convince Sammy that our case against John Gambino was an important one, a prosecution befitting testimony from a person of his stature. None of us mentioned that he was obligated to testify by his contract with the government. It was too early in the morning for that.

As we sat down to interview the diminutive mobster with the big nickname—"the Bull"—our FBI agent host opened with preliminaries, his solicitous tone conveying our sincere regret for stirring the great man so early.

"How you doin', Sammy? Need anything?"

"I'm doin' okay," came the reply. "Been playing a lotta handball. I could use some gloves for that. Better for the hands."

"Sure, Sammy, I'll take care of it."

"And don't get me some cheap-shit government gloves. Good handball gloves."

"Got it, Sammy."

I made a mental note about the gloves and we began our relationship.

Weeks later, I came back to the gloves. The Department of Justice has an obligation to disclose to the defense any information that might tend to undercut the credibility of a government witness—for example, by exposing bias or special treatment. Of course, defense lawyers had the mother lode of impeachment for Gravano: after living a life of crime and ending the lives of nearly two dozen other people, he had gotten a sweetheart deal. They could spend days exploring his bad acts and his powerful motive to please the government and protect his deal.

But I also needed to know if the government had given him stuff. So I asked him if he ever got those gloves for handball. He had. I asked if anyone from the government had given him anything else. Reading glasses. Anything else? Well, yes, the head of the FBI's New York office came to visit him at a safe house after he testified against John Gotti and the no-longer-Teflon Don was convicted. To mark the occasion, the FBI chief gave him a watch with the blue FBI seal reproduced on its face. Sammy beamed when he remembered the ceremony. I showed no reaction.

After we left Sammy, I told his FBI agent handler that I would need to disclose the gifts—especially the FBI watch—during his testimony at our Manhattan trial against John Gambino. And a war came. The FBI squad that handled Gravano and the Brooklyn federal prosecutors who first used him as a witness to take down Gotti already didn't trust us. He was their witness, after all. We were Manhattan feds constantly seeking to steal their cases from Brooklyn and Queens, two other parts of New York City that were their jurisdiction. They had reluctantly loaned us their star witness—to allow us to prove a murder they thought should have been prosecuted in Brooklyn anyway—and now we were going to embarrass him, and the FBI, over a stupid watch. The press would have a field day with the scene of the assistant director of the FBI giving a Bureau keepsake watch to a mobster. And Sammy was not going to like it, not one bit.

To be honest, the power imbalance extended to me. I really needed Gravano. He was the only way we could prove something awful John Gambino had done. He murdered an innocent man.

There had been a dispute and then a fistfight on the sidewalk in front of a Queens, New York, apartment building in an Italian neighborhood. Nobody knew what the fight was about. It was two neighbors fighting, maybe over loud music, maybe over a dog barking. The older guy was a well-known bully, but the younger man's punches ended up killing him. The cops didn't arrest anybody because nobody saw nothing, just an older guy lying on the sidewalk. But the older guy was named Frank Gambino. He wasn't a made guy, an official member of Cosa Nostra, but he was mobbed up. He was part of John Gambino's crew, an "associate," as they say. For that reason, somebody had to answer for this. You can't kill a guy in a Gambino crew and not pay for it.

John Gambino's crew investigated and concluded that a guy named Francesco Oliveri had done it. Armed with this knowledge, John and Joe Gambino went to see the family boss, John Gotti. They had a difficult relationship with Gotti, who found their "Sicilian wing" of the family a bit mysterious and threatening. Gotti didn't trust anybody—which was the only way he could stay alive, what with his having arranged the assassination of Paul Castellano, his careless and too-trusting predecessor, in front of a Manhattan steak house—but Gotti trusted the Sicilians even less than all those others he didn't trust. They had connections to the powerful Sicilian Mafia that Gotti—American-born, with ancestors from the Italian mainland—didn't have, and they spoke a language he didn't understand.

The Gambino brothers told Gotti what had happened to Frank Gambino and asked for permission to kill Oliveri in revenge. Gotti was confused by the request, although he didn't let them see his reaction. He was confused because he knew John Gambino's Sicilian wing had done plenty of "hits" without asking his permission.

There was no doubt John Gambino didn't need help killing people. What were they up to now, making a formal request? It was some kind of move by John Gambino. Gotti couldn't see the angles in the moment, but it was definitely a move. So, he made his own move. He gave his blessing and added something unprecedented: he wanted Gravano, the family's underboss—its vice president—to personally participate in the killing. His countermove was intended to show John Gambino, a dangerous man, that the leaders of the family weren't afraid of violence.

A Mafia hit team, including underboss Gravano and a key member of Gambino's crew, stalked Francesco Oliveri. They surveilled him. He had a routine, as most people do. Routines make killing easy. Early every Tuesday morning, Oliveri came out of his apartment building—the same building where Frank Gambino was beaten to death on the sidewalk—and moved his car. He did this to comply with New York City alternate-side parking regulations, which allowed street cleaners in Astoria, Queens, to do their work on Tuesday mornings. So, they would kill him on a Tuesday. After the boss's approval, the killers went on a Tuesday, but got there too late; Oliveri had already moved his car. He would live until another Tuesday.

The killers went back on Tuesday, May 3, 1988, and got there plenty early. The hit team was divided in two stolen cars, sitting at opposite ends of the block, communicating by walkie-talkie, as they waited for Francesco Oliveri to come move his car for the last time. A "clean" car was parked several blocks away, for the killers to switch to as they made their escape.

As Oliveri walked to his car on his final Tuesday, a member of the team stepped from a stolen car, walked up behind him, and shot him in the back of the head. A tiny explosion, one he never heard, propelled a cone-shaped piece of metal into his brain and Francesco Oliveri no longer existed. His lifeless body fell against a tree. His jacket snagged on the tree somehow, keeping him from falling flat on the ground. He stayed slumped against the tree, a sight Gravano remembered as he drove past in one of the two stolen cars. Several blocks away, the killers abandoned the hot cars, piled into the clean car, and were gone.

Francesco Oliveri would never again hurt a member of a Gambino crew. And a message had been sent. Except that Francesco Oliveri had never hurt a member of a Gambino crew, or anyone else, near as the FBI could tell. Yes, he lived in Frank Gambino's building, and he had surely suffered from Frank Gambino's bullying—as everybody did—but Francesco was a mild, middle-aged Ronzoni pasta factory worker. Neighbors said he didn't, and wouldn't, get in a fight, and he certainly wasn't strong enough to kill a man with his fists. The Gambino family investigation had identified the wrong guy. An innocent man was dead and snagged on a tree that cool May morning in Queens.

One of our defendants had been there that morning. He was a star in John Gambino's crew and a skilled killer, which is why John Gotti had been captured on tape in the widow's apartment calling him a "real man." In that hit man's top dresser drawer, the FBI found a bag containing a pistol with its serial number removed, hundreds of rounds of ammunition, rubber gloves, and a knit full-face black ski mask, with only mouth and eye holes. It was damning evidence of his role in Cosa Nostra. To deal with it during final arguments in our case, the mobster's lawyer casually plucked the mask from the evidence table and walked toward the jury box. Before the jurors entered, he had rolled it up so it now looked like a knit ski cap, which he waved dismissively, chastising the government for freaking out over "this knit hat, this cap."

In rebuttal, Pat Fitzgerald created courtroom legend. He pointed to the rolled-up, harmless "cap," then stunned the room, including me, by lifting his left leg and planting one black wingtip dress shoe on the railing of the jury box. He quickly rolled up the elevated pant leg, revealing first a black sock, then pasty-white hairy skin, then a knobby knee. He stopped and looked at the jurors, bare left leg in their faces. "If I ask you what I was wearing today, you wouldn't say, 'You walked in the court wearing shorts.'" He dropped his left leg to the floor, grabbed the cap by its top, and snapped his wrist, dangling the full face of the ski mask like a black knit Halloween jack-o'-lantern. He let it hang there for a moment, then rolled his pant leg back down and moved on to other arguments. I don't know what the jurors thought, because none of them married a case agent afterward. But I suspect there were high fives on the next break.

Gravano knew all about it—who requested the killing, who ordered it, who did it. Without him, nobody would answer for Francesco Oliveri. I needed Gravano, and loud voices said I was doing the wrong thing on the watch, that I was making a mountain out of an FBI gift-store molehill.

I took the coward's way out. Under pressure, both from Brooklyn and my own witness, I opted for the narrowest disclosure, one that the defense lawyers would likely miss. At trial, it went like this:

"During the time you have been in jail, has the government given you any personal items of any sort?"

"They have given me a watch and a pair of glasses."

"What is your understanding of the value of those things?"

"Together, probably about forty dollars, fifty dollars. I have no idea how much glasses cost, but the watch is about twenty dollars and I guess the glasses are about twenty, thirty dollars. It could be more. I'm not a hundred percent sure."

He was not asked a single question about it on cross-examination. Why would he be? It's not like it was an FBI watch given to him in a gratitude ceremony by the head of the New York FBI. And he forgot to mention the handball gloves. I let it go.

Three decades later, it doesn't feel right to me. I should have told Gravano he was going to testify that the head of the New York FBI gave him a watch. Sure, maybe the Brooklyn feds were right that it was cumulative with so much else to cross-examine him about. Maybe it was no big deal, but I had an obligation to ensure the defense lawyers knew the truth so they could decide how to handle it. I had a duty to be transparent, because my client wasn't Gravano, or the FBI, or even Francesco Oliveri's memory; my client was an institution that is committed to being just. There are clear lines, and if you have to spend hours debating whether you are too close to the line, you are. I was still learning.

Six years investigating and prosecuting cases in the Southern District of New York was exhilarating. From my colleagues, my supervisors, and my own mistakes, I learned that the truth could be inconvenient, embarrassing, and painful, but it was nonnegotiable. It was much more important than winning. And the source of that obligation to tell the truth couldn't be fear—of getting caught or looking bad. It had to be internal—a way of being, an orientation toward the work, and toward life, really. It helped that the office's culture made the commitment to truth a fierce point of pride. Of course, there was a youthful arrogance in that—we thought ourselves better than defense lawyers—but the pride made it a part of our identity. When I said something, or presented a witness who said something, it had to be what I believed, always. And that felt good.

The six years were also hard. I was tired and stressed. My dreams were filled with violence and crime. I cracked two molars grinding my teeth while I slept. I would get sick as a dog when a trial ended. And Patrice and I were starting a family, in a world without laptops, smartphones, or remote-work possibilities. As I sat in my office fifteen miles east of our half house, doing work I thought was really cool and important, Patrice's voice stayed in my head. She said it so often

I could quote her without a court transcript: "You can show these people that it's possible to be both a good lawyer and a good parent. You have to model that." When I would protest that my bosses might think less of me for leaving to be with my spouse and kids, she responded, "You don't want to work for anyone who doesn't respect your commitment to your family. And there are lots of prosecutors; our kids only have one dad."

So, I went home. Every night that I wasn't on the road meeting a witness, I was home in Maplewood to bathe the kids, to read them books. I would bring home work-related reading that didn't need a computer, then sit up and read after the little girls—the two oldest of what would end up being five kids—were asleep. I thought I was awesome. Until Patrice pointed out to me that my physical presence was not enough. "When you are here, you have to be *here,* not thinking about a case or a witness while you read *Goodnight Moon.* These little girls will be gone. Be here." She was right. I focused on the red balloon, the comb and brush and bowl full of mush. And the quiet old lady who was whispering, "Hush."

The mobsters and fake fur robbers would still be there when I was done.

PART TWO

Seeing the Reservoir

As I gained experience after my six years as a federal prosecutor in New York—first as a defense lawyer outside government and then as a supervisor when I returned to the Department of Justice—I realized that adherence to the values of the department added up to something: the faith and confidence of the people we served. As a leader responsible for supervising others and representing our work to a community, I started to see more clearly the value of the reservoir of trust and credibility, that invisible thing that helped us be believed, even in difficult circumstances. I also learned it was fragile—easily damaged by doubts about our integrity and our intentions. To earn trust, we needed to keep our promises and let the community see our hearts.

CHAPTER 9

FOR THE DEFENSE

The advocate has a duty to use legal procedure for the fullest
benefit of the client's cause . . .
AMERICAN BAR ASSOCIATION
MODEL RULES OF PROFESSIONAL CONDUCT

AFTER A SIX-MONTH TRIAL, the Gambino-case jury hung 11–1 on all the most serious charges, in suspicious circumstances; during final deliberations, the jurors slipped a note to the marshals alleging that one of the jury members likely had been paid off, but we couldn't find enough evidence to remove the guy at that point in the case. We were stuck with a corrupt juror. If he had been bought, it was because he sought out the Mob for a payday. The jury had been anonymous and carefully protected throughout the trial. It was heartbreaking. The defendants also knew they would never get that lucky again. All but one minor player pleaded guilty before retrial. That was just as well, because I was leaving.

Patrice had endured New York City for seven years because of me. I had reneged on our early deal that we would raise our family in Virginia. Because I wanted to be a federal prosecutor in Manhattan, Patrice and I had lived in the New Jersey suburbs, first in the shoebox apartment over the bike shop, then in our modest two-family-house rental. With our growing family, half of a house had become too cramped. We were headed south to raise our family in Richmond, Virginia, not far from the college where we met and fell in love. It was the right move for our family, but I was sad to leave the Southern District of New York, knowing I would never be back.

When we first started talking about moving away from New York, my plan was to try to transfer and be a Justice Department prosecutor—an Assistant United States Attorney—in Richmond, just as I had been in Manhattan. Patrice and I were at an awards ceremony in Washington for my work on the jewelry-district case, the one where we stopped the armed robbery by interviewing the junior mobster and prompting a flood of wiretapped conversations. She heard someone identify a man standing across the crowded room as the United States Attorney in Richmond, so she sidled up to me, shared this bit of intel, and urged me to go introduce myself to the guy: "He could hire you." I refused. There was no way I was going to buttonhole some stranger about a job at a Justice Department reception. As Patrice continued nudging me, very quietly, the man moved through the crowd and was gone.

That man would become my friend and colleague. By the time we were ready to move to Richmond after the Gambino case, he was out of office and the government wasn't hiring. I had to go to the private sector, and his law firm was one of only two in Richmond interested in speaking to me. They wanted me for their growing "product liability" practice, where they tried cases in defense of corporations accused of making or selling things that hurt people. Not my passion, but I needed a job. I went to the firm, where the people were lovely and the work was hard.

———

I represented a guy I believed was guilty, something experienced defense attorneys do all the time. It was a fraud case, and the client was
a charming and likable rogue, who had lied to various banks, credi-
tors, partners, and customers. Unfortunately for him, and his lovely,
pained-looking family, the Department of Justice had assembled
overwhelming evidence of his guilt, which he had never admitted, certainly not to his family and probably not even to himself.
I long ago figured out that the prospect of a defendant pleading
guilty turned mostly upon what he had told his family about the allegations. People are willing to forgo the sentence reduction that can
come with a guilty plea to avoid the pain of admitting a lie to a loved
one. My first question in assessing the chances of a plea has long
been, "What did he tell his family?"

I did my absolute best for the client, spending hours before trial
poring through the government's evidence, looking for something,
anything, that would help him. As I prepared to speak to the jury
in summation, I concluded that I could not ethically argue that my
client was innocent, because I didn't believe it. But I still had an obligation to do my best for him. So, I stood before that jury and argued
passionately that the United States of America had failed to meet its
burden of proving guilt beyond a reasonable doubt, a burden at the
core of ordered liberty and one the jury had sworn to uphold. With
a closing flourish invoking the wisdom of our founding fathers, and
doing my best to channel Gregory Peck in *To Kill a Mockingbird*, I
urged the members of the jury to do their duty and find my client
"not guilty." As I finished and eased into my chair at counsel table, my
client looped his arm around my shoulders and whispered in my ear,
"That was fantastic. I feel really good about this." In that moment, I
wanted to whisper, "Oh, God, man, you're going down like a box of
rocks," but I couldn't do it to him, despite his record of fraud, especially not with his wife sitting behind my shoulder—right there in

the front row. I felt sorry for him that he was even fooling himself. But he did go down like a box of rocks, for almost ten years in a federal prison. And his final check to our law firm bounced.

Even in civil cases, I learned painful lessons about my obligation as a private attorney to advocate for my client, and only my client. My firm sent me back to New York to try asbestos cases. They reasoned that I had come from New York and had tried many cases as a federal prosecutor, so it was a natural fit. Hardly.

The courtroom clerk's phone, sitting on a desk just below the judge's bench, rang loudly during the proceeding. *Brrriiing. Brrriiing.* The judge was on the bench, listening to New York lawyers argue, and the phone was ringing, loudly. Sitting in the audience, waiting for my case to be called, I seemed to be the only one who noticed. The clerk was sitting right there, inches from the loudly ringing phone, writing something with a pen. She got it on the third ring, whispering into the mouthpiece, one hand cupped to muffle any sound she might make, apparently so as not to interrupt the proceedings that had just endured 2.75 loud rings.

I've been in a lot of courtrooms. All over America, the clerk's phone blinks to indicate an incoming call. It's a small red or white light that only the clerk can see. Maybe one or two clerk phones in my career buzzed in an almost imperceptible way. And that made sense, because a ringing phone in a courtroom would both distract and detract from the solemnity of judicial proceedings.

Of course, this wasn't just any courtroom. This was New York City Housing Court, a room borrowed by a New York State trial judge who was presiding over asbestos cases, which had just become my specialty. My Richmond firm's client was a well-known industrial company that had never manufactured asbestos insulation, but used it in the 1940s and '50s to insulate large industrial equipment the company manufactured. Because the company feared being sued in thousands of cases if it paid any money to settle asbestos lawsuits, it didn't settle, ever. The problem for the company was that most companies that actually mined asbestos or manufactured insulation had long ago gone bankrupt or adopted a settlement strategy. That frequently left our client alone at the defense table in hundreds of lawsuits, many of which were in New York City.

There I sat, waiting for a status conference with the judge assigned to one of those asbestos lawsuits. As I looked around, it occurred to me that maybe the phone seemed so loud because the courtroom floor was made of linoleum tiles. They were uneven, with some corners missing. I tried to remember if I had ever seen a courtroom with linoleum tiles. Nope, just as I had never been in one with a ringing clerk's phone. I wondered if the tiles had asbestos in them, as older floor tiles frequently did. So long as the asbestos isn't disturbed, no problem, I thought, as I eyed those missing corners.

As the case ahead of mine droned on, I let my eyes drift to the judge's bench. I hadn't noticed it when I first came in, but above his head were large iron letters spelling out one of our national mottos—or trying to in the face of New York City's apparently small budget for replacement motto letters. The wall reminded all of us: IN OD WE RUST. I'm in hell, I thought. Just a few months ago, I was a senior Manhattan federal prosecutor handling big-time Mafia cases. Now I'm a Richmond lawyer standing on New York linoleum battling some poor guy dying of asbestos-related disease. It couldn't get worse. It did.

When my case was called, I took my place at counsel table. The plaintiff's lawyer spoke first. Then it was my turn. I rose, buttoned my jacket, stood straight, and identified myself in a clear voice, adding that I represented the defendant in this lawsuit. The judge squinted at me.

"Mr. Co-mey," he began, drawing out my two-syllable last name, as if trying to place me, "didn't you used to work down the street, at the United States Attorney's Office?"

"Yes, Your Honor, that's right," I replied in a level voice, concealing my pleasure at being recognized amid the indignity of an asbestos case.

His eyes moved from squint to a wide look of surprise, his head framed by OD and RUST. "How the mighty have fallen," he said.

With a weak smile, I said, "Thank you, Your Honor," and sat down. It couldn't get worse. But it did.

The court decided to change things up to encourage settlement. A judge would preside over a jury trial limited to damages only. That is, the jury would hear evidence about the plaintiff's illness and award an amount of money to compensate him for that illness. But nobody would get the chance to argue it wasn't their fault. There would be a later trial to determine who was responsible for paying that money if all the parties didn't settle. The judge's thinking was that companies, like the one I represented, were more likely to settle a case if they knew exactly what their financial exposure was, if they had a hard, jury-awarded number to work with. My client, which maintained that it had no responsibility because it had never made an asbestos product, was not going to settle. But if you were ever going to settle, this might be a good time.

The plaintiff was a genial man in his early seventies who had worked for years around various asbestos products, first in the navy and later in big factories, where he repaired machinery. He was sick with a disease caused only by asbestos—pleural mesothelioma. It is a rare and universally fatal ailment of unique cruelty, in which the thin lining that encases the lungs gradually thickens until it is like the rind of an orange, suffocating and killing the patient. There is no cure. There are few worse ways to die.

Given what the judge had done, my job was not to argue to the jury that my client could not have been the source of the asbestos that was killing this poor man. I had good facts there: as much as we all felt for the plaintiff, the evidence showed it wasn't our fault. But I couldn't say such a thing. No, my job was to use all my skill as an advocate to limit the amount of money the jury judged this man's life to be worth. Whatever the plaintiff said his suffering and life were worth, my job was to knock that number down. You see, it could get worse.

The evidence consisted of medical testimony about the awfulness of mesothelioma and the nightmare that awaited this gentle man and his wife sitting there in the front row, and their children and grandchildren. He took the witness stand to tell the jury of his love for his family and for life, and of his fear for what awaited him. Late at night in my Manhattan hotel room, I was awakened by nightmares in which I couldn't breathe. I called Patrice to tell her I was trapped in something terrible. Then, the next morning, I stood in front of a jury and argued about what it was all worth, what life itself is worth. I stood there aching for this man and, as gently as I could, abiding by my obligation to represent my client—which I believed was not actually responsible for his agony, although I was prohibited from saying so. I suggested to the jury that eight million dollars was too much and four or five might be more appropriate. My heart was not in it. I felt I was losing a piece of my soul. I don't know what the jurors thought of me, but they awarded a number that was slightly below what the poor man's lawyer requested. Everyone lost, him most of all.

As a change of pace, the firm assigned me something different. I was sent to the mountains of western Virginia to argue that an old man did not have a different kind of lung disease. We represented a railroad that was facing a raft of cases alleging that former freight train employees had silicosis, a lung disease caused by airborne sand. Freight train engines drop small amounts of sand on the tracks to help them gain traction as they start to pull a big train. I had seen these little piles around rail yards; they look like a kid knocked over a beach pail. Silicosis disease didn't kill people, but it made it hard to breathe. It was most common among sandblasters or mine workers, but former railroaders were saying they got it from years of those little sand piles blowing around rail yards.

The old man in this case worked and lived in Clifton Forge, a three-square-mile town of four thousand souls in the Alleghany Highlands, hard against the Jackson River. For decades, Clifton Forge had been a rail hub. Coal trains coming from the west and headed downriver to the ships in Newport News and Norfolk would be rearranged or "switched" in the hump yard at Clifton Forge. Yard engines would push freight cars over a small artificial hill—the hump—which would give them momentum to glide onto any of the side tracks the yard operator chose in order to form new trains. Once a collection of coal cars had been "built" into a train, a locomotive would hook up and begin to move tons of coal toward the final destination. To get going from a standing start, the locomotive would drop sand on the track to help the wheels grip. Railroad employees would be working throughout the yard, hooking up cars and directing yard engines.

I met the retired old guy when I took his deposition. He seemed grouchy to me, not like the pleasant dying man in New York who haunted my dreams. This guy seemed pissed off at everyone. Years later, I would be reminded of him by Clint Eastwood's character in the 2008 movie *Gran Torino*. I didn't buy the grouchy guy's story. He had worked in the yard for only a small part of his career and he was a heavy smoker. It was going to be easy to argue he didn't get lung disease from being around trains. And my client had experts who would testify that the little piles of sand don't fly around anyway. He was working near trains, for heaven's sake, not sandblasters.

Still, trying this case in Clifton Forge was going to be an away game. My client had been steadily cutting rail jobs there, replacing people with computers and machines. As a result, the little town in the mountains was dying. The jury was going to be made up of Clifton Forge residents who would be asked to decide between the big bad railroad and a neighbor in his seventies who said the rail yard made him sick. An away game.

As if to remind everyone of my client's role in the life of the shrinking town, Clifton Forge's two-story redbrick courthouse—with the clock tower and grand front columns—was next to the rail yard. Literally, it was the building closest to the hump, just across a parking lot out the back door. In the warm Virginia spring, the windows in the second-floor courtroom were open during the trial and I could hear trains groaning and screeching all day. The jury sat in an odd configuration, arranged in a two-tiered box directly in front of the judge's bench, looking away from him toward the witness stand, where those testifying stared directly at the jury and judge. The lawyers' tables were on either side of the room, against the walls. The judge towered over the courtroom from a third level, staring at the back of the jurors' heads. Every one of those heads said they knew the plaintiff, but could still be fair and impartial. They also all had friends and relatives who had worked for the railroad, but could be fair and impartial. I had no chance.

Both sides put on their cases. I argued that the railroad hadn't made the guy sick; he didn't work there long enough and, besides, the experts said the sand didn't fly around; it stayed in the little piles next to the tracks. I gave it my best shot. When the jury left to deliberate, I went to the men's room. In the cramped old courthouse, it was the same bathroom the jury used, but the court clerk assured me it was safe to use quickly. The bathroom had a single, tall, double-hung window. It was high in the wall, with the lower half blacked out for privacy. The upper part was dropped down so the top half of the window was open. I was tall enough to stand and watch the impressive activity of the rail yard outside and hear the trains through the screen. Trains are so cool, I thought. I'm going to miss this place. As I started to turn toward the door, I noticed the tops of the two window pieces. The dark metal surfaces were coated in fine sand, something I had just spent hours arguing was impossible. I paused for a moment, then leaned and blew it all out through the screen.

The jury came back and sided with the railroad, which was thrilled by my unexpected victory. But it had nothing to do with me, or my slimy little move blowing sand out of the bathroom. The jury knew Clifton Forge far better than I did, or my experts. They would have laughed at the sand on the sill. They knew sand flew everywhere near the rail yard. They also knew the retired guy—they had delivered his paper, or served him at the diner, or stood behind him at the grocery store—and they knew he was a complete jerk. They were never going to give that bastard a dime.

I had to get away from this work. I ached to return to the Department of Justice, where I was required to only make arguments I believed in and to represent an institution that belonged to the American people. I didn't ever want to be tempted again to blow sand off the windowsill.

I wanted to be in a place where, as the Supreme Court explained long ago, my duty is not to win, "but that justice shall be done."

The federal hiring freeze lifted, and I got the chance to return to the government as a federal prosecutor in Richmond, with the United States Attorney's Office for the Eastern District of Virginia. I liked my colleagues at the firm, and had become very close with some. In a gesture Patrice and I have never forgotten, the firm paid for our infant son's funeral when nine-day-old Collin died of a bacterial infection. They packed the church for his service. These were good people. It wasn't them, it was the work. Defense lawyering is essential to our system of justice, and really hard, but I needed work that meant more to me. Prosecuting federal criminal cases was not without its ethics issues—I once had to reprimand a New York cop during testimony preparation after he erupted at me, "Christ, man, just tell me what you want me to say"—and making complicated cases required dances with deeply flawed human witnesses, but the work was about finding the truth, above all else.

Private practice left me with a deep appreciation for the importance of clients having good lawyers with a duty of loyalty to them alone. But it also reminded me how different the obligations were for prosecutors with the Department of Justice, who had a different kind of client, one that insisted they always tell the truth and keep their promises. After three years away from it, I was headed back into government to represent that client, the people of the United States. And in Richmond, the work was more interesting than I ever expected.

CHAPTER 10

WEIRD SEX

Promises are the uniquely human way of ordering the future,
making it predictable and reliable to the extent that this is
humanly possible.
HANNAH ARENDT

LOTS OF PEOPLE PROBABLY HAD weird sex in Richmond.
But they didn't talk about it. Until a prostitute told the cops that a
well-known Virginia politico had hired her to do cocaine and have
sex with his wife for her birthday while the birthday girl was tied,
blindfolded, to a stairway railing. And it got weird from there. But
the case really got its start when I met Bob Trono, a local Virginia
prosecutor, who ran a regional drug task force handling cases that
spanned jurisdictional lines of the counties making up the Richmond
metro area. Bob was also designated as a part-time federal prosecutor, a Special Assistant United States Attorney, because many of his
cases led to interstate drug rings and became federal cases.

I liked Bob immediately because he didn't fit the mold of the
typical federal prosecutor. For starters, he drove a tricked-out, soft-
champagne-colored BMW with dark, tinted windows that had
been seized from a drug dealer. One day, as I slid into the passenger

seat of his Beemer with the killer rims to drive to a meeting, I noticed he had a semiautomatic pistol jammed muzzle down between his seat and the center console. I soon found out why that made complete sense.

I have only missed Halloween with my children once in my life. The five Comey kids covered about twenty-five years of trick-or-treating. I was not there October 31, 1996. I wasn't there because some drug dealers wanted to kill Bob. A reliable informant had told the police that, to derail a case Bob was prosecuting against some big Richmond drug dealers, the dealers had hired a killer from New York to shoot Bob as he walked out of a local county courthouse following a hearing on the case. The Richmond law enforcement community joined arms to protect Bob, providing around-the-clock security for him and his family while we tried to stop the planned hit. I attended a strategy session at which Bob expressed frustration that this was consuming so many resources and frightening his family. "Give me a vest," he said. "Lemme walk out of the courthouse and when the shooter shows himself, SWAT takes him out."

I remember thinking, That's the stupidest idea I've ever heard. I kinda like this guy. His plan was rejected. Instead, I spent Halloween night in a local jail, confronting a just-arrested suspect who knew the shooter's identity. We polygraphed the guy and he showed deception on that critical question. With his lawyer's consent, I stood over him and brought everything I had—cajoling him, reasoning with him, and threatening him with life in federal prison. I'm not a shouter, but I shouted. None of it worked. He wouldn't crack. I don't know whether he was too afraid to talk, or really didn't know who the shooter was, despite the polygraph—a "test" I was learning to treat with great skepticism. But the shooter never came. Every year on Halloween, Bob and I exchange messages. Mine is about how I missed Halloween to save his life. His is about my failure as an interrogator.

After I either did or did not save Bob's life, we became closer colleagues and good friends. I started working to convince my boss, the
United States Attorney, to hire Bob as a full-time Assistant United
States Attorney because he was a great trial lawyer and his local contacts
and sources would be valuable to the feds. That's where it got weirder.

Bob and the detectives assigned to support his state drug work talked
to the prostitute and started to develop a drug case against the prominent Richmond political figure. Because Bob knew I was interested
in seeing whether there were public corruption cases to be brought in
Richmond—a state capital where there hadn't been a corruption case
in living memory—Bob brought his information to me at the U.S.
Attorney's Office and I invited the FBI in to join the investigative
team. The subject was someone who had served as chief of staff to
both a recent Virginia governor and the current mayor of Richmond.
He was a colorful figure, married to a Tennessee retail-foods heiress.
But as colorful as he was, the allegations were outlandish and seemed
unlikely to go anywhere. The early information was that this guy
was supplying cocaine to people—men and women—who agreed to
participate in sex acts with him and his heiress wife. In Richmond?
Can't be. But there was enough there to take a look. So, we looked.
And couldn't look away.

We interviewed a series of attractive women and men in their twenties, all of whom told a similar story. Our subject had befriended
the woman or man, invited him or her to his lovely home on the
bluffs above the James River, served drinks and then cocaine, and
the evening ended with all manner of combinations, involving both
husband and heiress wife. One woman told of an early date with our
subject where he served pizza. As she bit into her first slice, she felt

something crunch. When he briefly left the room, she lifted the cheese and saw chopped-up blue pills lying beneath. When we asked her what she did next, she replied, "I didn't eat any more pizza." But she kept seeing him. "He was a lot of fun," she explained.

Despite their naïveté, our witnesses were desperately afraid of being ruined by publicity. They knew any charges brought against our subject would be big news in Richmond. The investigators and I quietly met one witness at an out-of-town hotel. He was a tall, handsome former star high school athlete, now in his late twenties. He explained that he was still married to his high school sweetheart, a former cheerleader. He acknowledged that he had gotten drugs from our subject, and engaged in complicated sex acts. His own wife had no idea what he was into. He then paused and leveled his eyes at me. "That's the truth. But if you ever ask me to tell it in a courtroom I will put a bullet in my brain first." I had no doubt that he meant it. I paused and then made a promise: "I will do everything I possibly can to protect you." His eyes moist and locked on me, he slowly and silently nodded his head again and again. I couldn't tell whether the nods meant he was grateful for my commitment or certain I was full of shit and he was going to have to commit suicide. "I promise," I added. He continued nodding.

To keep that promise to him and the others, we had to find a way to bring this case so it would end quickly, without a trial. I drafted an indictment that included a variety of drug distribution counts, and included the allegation that much of the cocaine was exchanged for group sexual activity, but didn't name any of our witness-participants. Maybe mentioning group sex in a federal indictment wouldn't have been shocking in Manhattan, but we weren't in New York. It caused a big storm in Richmond and, rather than capitulate, the defendant hired Richmond's most aggressive criminal defense attorney, who immediately began attacking the case in the media and attempting to frighten our still-unidentified witnesses, telling reporters they were a "plate of cockroaches." We were in for a fight, and would have to make hard decisions about calling witnesses out of the shadows. The case might fall apart because we didn't want to ruin these young people.

There had to be some way to put more pressure on this bad guy. It was clear that his wife's money was paying for his lifestyle and his obnoxious lawyer. Even for the politico's toupee. In a meeting with the investigative team, I asked whether her wealthy parents in Tennessee had any idea what this guy had gotten their daughter into. Nobody knew. I asked whether it made sense to send an investigator to Tennessee just to knock on the door of their mansion and ask what they know about their son-in-law. The team liked that. Don't tell them anything; just ask questions. You never know what we might learn. Even if we didn't learn anything, it might heat his world up a bit, create some motion in his backfield. And it's only an eight-hour drive. So, we sent Detective Sam Richardson, a legendary Richmond police detective and bear of a man, whose sideline was running one of the city's leading barbecue establishments. I can still hear his voice on the phone from Tennessee.

"Are you sitting down? You better sit down."

"What, Sam? What did you find?"

"I found her parents' place."

"Good. What's it like?" I asked, picturing Tara from *Gone with the Wind*.

"It backs up to a post office parking lot."

"What?"

"It's tiny," he said. "It's a dump. It's smaller than my house. These people have no money at all. None. It's a lie. She ain't no heiress. It's all a fraud."

It was over. We quickly brought a raft of federal fraud charges against both husband and wife, based on the "heiress" lies they had told to banks, brokers, investors, and others. Armed with arrest warrants and a search warrant, the investigative team descended on their home along the James River at dawn. She was cooperative. He pretended to be having a stroke and was unresponsive, until EMTs began to push a breathing tube down his throat. He snapped upright, revived.

Despite the impressive recovery, he began manifesting the symptoms of a very unusual stroke, speaking in a slurred voice but dragging his left leg and his *right* arm. It became known around the courthouse as the first "diagonal stroke" in medical history. He walked into the courtroom with that odd, opposite gait. The presiding federal judge, who had been concerned, understandably, that I was being too aggressive with the earlier drug charges, now saw the full picture. He looked down at the defendant and lectured him: "Now that the government has dropped the other shoe, you give me this *Rain Man* routine. I'm not having it." He ordered the defendant jailed and medically evaluated before trial, without his hairpiece. There had been no stroke. He quickly hired a new lawyer and negotiated a deal to plead guilty and cooperate. We reached out to our terrified witnesses and told them we were done, and they would never hear from us again. We kept that promise.

Maybe it was something in the James River's water that brought great cases to the big houses on the river bluffs. Just a half mile downriver from the politico and the fake heiress lived another prominent Richmond transplant, Baron Otto von Bressensdorf. The silver-haired founder of Lyons Capital owned the eleven-thousand-square-foot Tudor Revival mansion named Doolough Lodge by its original owners in 1920, an homage to their ancestral home in County Clare, Ireland. An application for the National Register of Historic Places noted the "steeply pitched slate-clad gable and hipped roofs, projecting castellated bays, wooden casement windows, and tall brick chimneys with terra-cotta pots. . . . Interestingly, the rectangular-shaped house is set with its short end to the river where a fieldstone terrace provides a commanding view." Doolough Lodge suited the baron.

Each morning, he made the short drive in his Rolls-Royce to Lyons Capital's richly decorated offices, adorned with mementos of a life well lived and well rewarded. The baron was not only of royal German ancestry but also the scion of a European banking family going back hundreds of years. His family's generations of success had been interrupted only by the war years in Germany, when he was forced to flee the Nazis and risked his life to join Italian resistance fighters bent on killing Hitler.

After the war, he gained the trust of American authorities by using his financial genius to help administer Marshall Plan funds. The connections he gained from that effort helped him rebuild the family business from the smoking crater of Hamburg. Once rebuilt, that business—which became Lyons Capital—consisted of a network of hundreds of agents around the world, just waiting for the opportunity to arrange funding for worthy entrepreneurial projects. Much of the funding came from the baron's equally impressive connections to European pension funds and other Continental sources of capital. He would travel periodically to Europe with a briefcase full of American projects needing funding and lay these before his European peers, who were hungry to invest in Lyons's clients.

After the baron emigrated to the United States, his star only continued to rise. He and Lyons Capital first settled in Los Angeles. Despite being a continent away, the baron continued to be well regarded by the United States government in Washington. In fact, President George H. W. Bush honored him with the nation's highest civilian award, the Presidential Order of Merit. He was also one of only a very few individuals to be honored while still living by having their names inscribed on the wall at the Ronald Wilson Reagan Eternal Flame of Freedom in Washington. It was his continual need to be in Washington—where he was a member of the National Republican Senatorial Committee—that led him to relocate Lyons from Los Angeles to Richmond in 1993; as an added benefit, the time-zone change made it easier to deal with his many European business contacts.

In both Los Angeles and Richmond, Lyons was an extraordinarily successful venture capital firm, finding funding for at least 70 percent—and perhaps as high as 90 percent—of the firm's clients. It had found funding for a wide variety of ventures, from golf courses to medical devices to storage facilities, and had funded deals as large as hundreds of millions of dollars. Of particular note was the fact that it had handled hundreds of transactions without a single complaint or lawsuit by a disgruntled client. While the baron was not free to disclose the name of any prior client—due to understandable concerns about privacy—he was at liberty to provide a list of references who could be contacted, including a Los Angeles accountant and two New York securities attorneys, all of whom were familiar with Lyons's impressive success rate and impeccable reputation.

Needless to say, the baron could not run an enterprise as far-flung and successful as Lyons by himself. He was assisted by a large staff, but his right and left hands were the two vice presidents of Lyons: his spouse, Elena Bisheff von Bressensdorf, who handled sales and marketing, and Barbara Lichtenberg, who was a legally trained securities expert in charge of assisting clients with developing first-class offering memoranda to be presented to Lyons's funding network. Once completed—and the offering memoranda were usually ready in 60 days—it would be only about another 90 to 150 days before Lyons's marketing department found funding for the client's project.

And all an entrepreneur with an idea needed in order to secure Lyons's help was to pay a modest advance fee of between ten thousand and thirty thousand dollars (depending on ability to pay). Lyons would use this fee to support the extensive underwriting and legal efforts of Lichtenberg and her staff, which were necessary to create a suitable offering and to present it to the usual array of European pension funds. Once the project received funding, Lyons would be entitled to a percentage of the total amount funded as well as an additional fixed fee.

If the potential client was not in a position to pay the up-front fee for Lyons's full efforts, the firm also developed another vehicle—the 2500 or 2000 program—through which a client could obtain a small, but valuable, part of the Lyons experience. For twenty-five hundred or two thousand dollars, Lyons would provide a list of funding sources who shared the client's area of interest and had invested in similar projects. While those paying the smaller fee would not receive the benefits of Lyons's underwriting and full-court marketing effort, they would receive preprinted mailing labels so the client could send his own solicitation to these potential investors.

Nearly every word in the preceding eight paragraphs—other than the awesome house and the amount of money charged hundreds of poor saps looking for financing—was a lie. It was all a fantastic fraud. The baron was not a baron, unless you count his having personally typed "Barone" before his name on his Italian birth certificate. Otto did see wartime service, but it was with the German Luftwaffe's Hermann Goering Panzer Division, before he was captured in 1945 by American forces. He was discharged from the defeated German army in 1945 and worked in the insurance industry before emigrating to the United States with his longtime associate and insurance co-worker, Barbara Lichtenberg. In Los Angeles, the two were joined by Elena, who had a cosmetology license.

The Presidential Order of Merit was a political token he received for donating less than five hundred dollars to the Republican Party; tens of thousands of others were similarly "honored" by the Republican Party. His name was indeed inscribed on the wall at the Reagan Eternal Flame of Freedom, located at Republican National Headquarters, along with six hundred others who each gave one thousand dollars—while still very much alive—to the Republican Party. A political contribution likewise got him designated a member of the National Republican Senatorial Committee.

The lies about Lyons's operation were less entertaining but more egregious. Lyons had a success rate at or very close to zero; even Barbara Lichtenberg, at her arrest, could recall only one deal that ever closed at Lyons. There were no funding sources waiting to gobble up Lyons deals. There was no exclusive worldwide Lyons selling network. In most cases, that particular fraud was of little consequence, because very few projects actually made it past Lichtenberg's "underwriting" process, which took many, many months at best and wore down even the most enthusiastic clients. Those clients who actually succeeded in getting Lichtenberg to approve an offering memorandum to market received no funding and their projects died, along with dozens of other "offering memoranda" in boxes at Lyons's offices. Lyons had a hard time retaining employees, who quickly figured out they were part of a scam. Early in his tenure, a young salesperson overheard a colleague ask, "I wonder what the heck we are going to do when the FBI comes through the window."

There had been endless complaints and lawsuits, but somehow the baron pressed on for years and found new victims. The "references" were a corrupt Los Angeles accountant paid $12.50 for each reference and two equally corrupt New York lawyers, both of whom were paid not for legal work, but for references. All these references simply told clients what Otto told them to say—that Lyons was hugely successful at finding funding. Hundreds of people were ripped off, losing their advance fee and their dream of their own business. The baron raked in millions, which he used to support Doolough Lodge and his lifestyle as a "Richmond royal."

It finally ended in January 1998, just as the politico and the heiress from up the river were headed, well, up the river, to prison. Early one morning, the FBI arrested the von Bressensdorfs at the Lodge. Like all great fraudsters, they went to trial, where they put on a good show but were convicted by a jury and dogged prosecutors from my office. They continued battling on appeal, where I represented the government, before finally spending ten years in federal prison. Doolough Lodge and the Rolls-Royce were sold at auction by the United States Marshals Service.

In Richmond in the 1990s, we weren't just chasing fraudsters with nice houses overlooking the James River. We were also engaged in an aggressive effort to use federal gun prosecutions—and the long prison terms that came with them—to drive down gun violence by making criminals think of their guns as a liability. The work mattered because human life had become cheap in large parts of the city.

I was driving with the deputy police chief, on our way to a breakfast meeting. He got a call over the radio and asked if I minded if he made a quick stop at a crime scene. No problem. The "scene" wasn't much of one. A new-model pickup truck sat at a stop sign, its engine still running. It was a cold day, but the driver's window was rolled down. The woman looked to be about forty and was leaning back against the seat headrest, as if she had dozed off at the stop sign. She was sleeping so soundly that her mouth was open. But she would never awaken. I could see a small red hole in her left temple and a large exit wound on her right. She stopped to buy drugs on her way to work, got into some kind of dispute with the dealer, and he shot his customer in the head, right there, in daylight, at the spot where he sold drugs to addicts in cars. Killing a customer in your own store. It made no sense at all, like most of Richmond's killings. Stopping that violence consumed law enforcement.

We were trying to use the more severe penalties available in federal court to literally scare drug dealers and felons away from guns. The gun had become an article of clothing in Richmond; a felon or drug dealer gave it no more thought before going out than their socks and shoes. They didn't fear what the local Richmond prosecutors and courts might do to them. Many of these criminals weren't well educated, but they were very good at cost-benefit analyses. We wanted to use the prospect of federal prosecution, which often meant a mandatory five-year sentence, to force them to think, and leave the gun home or hide it nearby. If criminals feared getting caught with a gun—and serving a long federal sentence far from home—we would have fewer murders in Richmond, a place where a planned killing was rare and murders were most often the product of a dispute that ratcheted up to the most lethal outcome. Impose stiff federal sentences and advertise that widely, and you would reduce illegal gun carrying. Reduce the rate at which felons and drug dealers carried guns, and you would reduce the murder rate.

An aggressive enforcement effort, especially one focused on the highest-crime areas of the city, would be controversial, unless the good people of those neighborhoods understood what we were doing and why. The gun enforcement effort in Richmond locked up a lot of people of color, and helped reduce violence. And it did those things without resistance in the Black community because law enforcement leaders offered transparency. All of us involved in the effort devoted enormous effort to showing ourselves and explaining our work. We did that in person, on TV, in the newspaper. We did it in churches, town halls, and recreation centers. We didn't just roll in and lock up a lot of young Black men. We enlisted an entire community in the effort, based on a shared goal of stopping the killing. It worked. Violent crime dropped and community support rose. Effective law enforcement depends upon public trust. And that trust depends upon transparency.

The lessons of Richmond stayed with me throughout my career. As the leader of a public institution, I had to address doubt about the integrity of the work or risk a corrosive doubt about justice.

Despite its crime problems, Richmond was wonderful, and Patrice and I were planning to stay forever. We found what we had been looking for—good public schools and a nice and relatively inexpensive house in a safe neighborhood. And then 9/11 happened.

We had five children by then, aged one to thirteen. After the terror attacks, President George W. Bush needed to appoint a new United States Attorney in Manhattan, one who would be acceptable to the spectrum of feuding New York political leaders, and one who knew that office and terrorism investigations, which I had handled in Virginia before 9/11. Although I hadn't applied, I was the pick. It was an emotional decision for me and Patrice to go back to New York, for a reason few knew: our son Collin was buried in Richmond, not far from our house. We had also purchased burial plots for ourselves, just beside him, and believed we would spend our lives in Richmond and then stay, forever. Instead, we would go to New York, where the World Trade Center site still smoked. I would lead my old office, where 250 prosecutors were handling hundreds of cases, ranging from terrorism to violent crime to corporate fraud. My head spun at the thought.

PART THREE

Protecting the Reservoir

When I became a senior leader in the Department of Justice, I real-
ized my job was to protect the reservoir of trust and credibility, by insist-
ing that our work be evenhanded and nonpartisan—and seen that way
by all Americans. A commitment to the truth, coupled with transpar-
ency about success and failure, fostered that indispensable trust. Telling
the whole truth sometimes angered other people in government, because
mistakes are painful, but being open and honest about them earned the
trust of those we served. I also learned that the department could be led
by political appointees without becoming a partisan institution, but that
we needed the president of the United States to help us guard the reser-
voir. Sometimes we got that support. Other times we didn't, and the cost
to Justice was high.

CHAPTER II

THE IMPOSTOR

Your responsibility in your several districts for law enforcement
and for its methods cannot be wholly surrendered to Washington,
and ought not to be assumed by a centralized
Department of Justice.
ATTORNEY GENERAL ROBERT H. JACKSON
ADDRESS TO U.S. ATTORNEYS, 1940

I WAS BACK IN NEW YORK. And Katie Couric had tiny TV furniture. I suppose it could have been the early hour, but it sure seemed small to me. I was in my first year as the United States Attorney in Manhattan and up at dawn so I could hit all the morning news shows. We had made arrests in an enormous identity fraud case—the biggest ever, to that point—in which tens of thousands of Americans had their credit records stolen and sold to criminals. It was a cool story, sure to be of interest to the morning shows. We didn't tell anyone at the Department of Justice in Washington, because if we had, they would have stolen the story so the attorney general could announce it. And I wanted to build my public profile to make it harder for them to mess with me and my office.

———

I needed the public profile because I didn't have anything else to use as a shield.

In 1906, the reform-minded president, Theodore Roosevelt, wanted to change the U.S. Attorney's office for the Southern District of New York. That office, which in its original form opened in 1789, was older than the Department of Justice itself. The court in which the office's prosecutors worked was known as the Mother Court, because it began operating weeks before the U.S. Supreme Court. The Southern District of New York had been around since the founding of the country, and Roosevelt didn't like what it had become—a place of political patronage, uninterested in troubling the powerful.

Roosevelt changed that with a single appointment, of Henry L. Stimson, a young, Harvard-educated Wall Street lawyer, who would go on to serve as secretary of state and secretary of war for four presidents of both parties. Among them was a brand-new chief executive, Harry Truman, who needed to know about the atomic bomb. ("I think it is very important that I should have a talk with you as soon as possible on a highly secret matter," Stimson wrote his new boss.)

In the Southern District of New York, he immediately fired people. They were hacks, in his estimation, careerist or corrupt or both. He replaced them with recent graduates from top law schools, whom he wanted only for a few years, after which they would go work for fancy law firms and be replaced by other idealistic and talented young lawyers. There are few moments of true pivot in the life of institutions, but the Southern District pivoted in 1906. In the words of one of the district's judges, "Henry L. Stimson changed the office of United States Attorney. He created the model of competence, integrity and professionalism that has set the standard for prosecutors ever since."

With Stimson, a culture was founded. Politics were disdained. Academic achievement was prized. The lawyers were known for being better—smarter, more principled, harder working—than those in other federal offices, especially at the main Department of Justice in Washington. And so began the forever war with Main Justice.

Some of the snobbery was justified. On average, our lawyers wrote better, worked harder, and thought more creatively than those in other places. On average. There were duds in the Southern District and plenty of great federal prosecutors in other offices, with their own traditions of independence. But it really was true that the place disdained politics and prized the independence of 1906. It was drilled into you during the application process, reinforced by your supervisors, and policed by the many federal judges and powerful law firm partners who were alumni of "the Office," as it was known. Henry Stimson left a bequest, held in trust, and our job was to protect it. And the most important way to preserve and protect it was to never forget that Washington was political and that was bad. People in D.C. always asked, "How will this look?" before they ever asked, "What is true?" That world was one of appearances, spin, damage control, popularity, politics.

Main Justice never saw it that way. It was absurd that one of the ninety-four United States Attorney's offices had such an attitude, seeing itself as separate and apart, above the political. The attorney general and the department's senior staff at Main Justice are in charge of the department; the president picked them to be in charge, just as the president picked the U.S. Attorneys. The pompous Southern District of New York—calling itself "the Southern District," as if everyone should know the rest—was led by just another presidential appointee and should be brought to heel. There are eleven other districts with "Southern" in their names.

The struggle continued through every presidential administration and then again when a new president appointed new leadership at Main Justice and in Manhattan. Things always heated up when new administrations arrived; after all the snobbery and slights from New York, that's when Main Justice was going to change things, to assert itself, to change the traditions to reflect the constitutional design of presidential control over the executive branch. But sometimes the Office managed to resist even the normal political transition following an election. Democratic appointee Robert Morgenthau, who started as U.S. Attorney under John F. Kennedy and was reappointed by Lyndon Johnson, famously refused to resign when the Republican Richard Nixon became president. And Morgenthau's power and influence were so great—he was the scion of one of America's great families—that the Nixon administration avoided direct conflict and chose to starve him out, cutting off all funding to the Southern District (of New York). Veterans of that siege remembered conserving precious legal pads and pencils until Morgenthau finally relented.

I had wonderful parents, but I was not from a great American family in the same sense. I had not been a powerful government official and likely future senator or mayor, as Rudy Giuliani was when he became U.S. Attorney. I didn't have the relationships in the legal community and with prominent New Yorkers that my predecessor, Mary Jo White, had built during a career spent in the city. I was a career prosecutor from Richmond, Virginia, whom the Bush administration chose to replace White because I had once worked in the Office, I had done terror cases, and I was acceptable to both the governor, a Republican, and the senior senator, a Democrat. I was the relationship everyone settled for.

I was still in Richmond when Mary Jo called me. Main Justice was making its move. They were planning to send a lawyer to argue an appeal in one of "our" cases in Manhattan. It had to be stopped. It wasn't done. A dangerous precedent. Lawyers from Washington must be kept out of "our" district. I loved Mary Jo, but all the "our" business confused me. *She* was the United States Attorney, for two more months; I was a low-level prosecutor in another district with a large and growing impostor complex over this whole thing after being announced as her replacement. "They won't listen to me because I'm on the way out," she explained. "You need to call Ted Olson and stop this. If you don't, it will be a terrible way for you to start."

Olson was the solicitor general of the United States and a giant of the American legal profession. I was not either of those things, and it took me a while to build up the courage to call him. He had no idea who I was, but listened on the phone as I told him my sad story, of how he was going to make things hard for me, about the ghost of Henry L. Stimson. He was ready for the pitch. He knew the history better than I, and laid out instances over the preceding decades in which Main Justice lawyers had occasionally ventured into "our" district when the attorney general thought it was necessary. Normally, he explained, it isn't necessary because your people are so good, but this is a specialized area and the lawyer from Main has done this same argument all over the country. You will be able to distinguish this case. It won't hurt you. It won't open any floodgate. Stimson's ghost won't come for you. I called Mary Jo to tell her I had failed.

I had been sad to leave the Manhattan U.S. Attorney's office for Richmond in 1993, after the Gambino case. Patrice knew I was sad because I said it, constantly. One day in the car I whined, "Now I will never get the chance to be the U.S. Attorney in Manhattan." I actually said that. She remembers it, too, because I held up her reply eight years later, when I was asked to go back and replace Mary Jo

White. To stop the whining, she said, "I would come back for that."
It was a throwaway line, something to cheer me up. It cost her nothing because there was no chance that somebody from outside New
York would be made the United States Attorney in Manhattan. Since
1789, it had never happened. She might as well have said, "I would
come back for you to play the Jean Valjean role in *Les Misérables* on
Broadway." Empty words at empty tables.

I went up to Manhattan alone in December 2001 to begin over-
lapping with Mary Jo White, leaving Patrice in Richmond with
the five kids. The government found me a temporary apartment on
John Street in lower Manhattan. Empty space was easy to find in
lower Manhattan immediately after the attack on the World Trade
Center. Space in the suburbs was a different story, as families who
could afford to move began streaming away from Manhattan. We
wanted a house that could fit the seven of us, in a suburban neighborhood with good public schools. Oh, and we didn't have much
money and couldn't afford much of a down payment.

Patrice took a house-hunting trip with her best friend from Virginia
and was shocked at how tight the market was. She finally found a
house in Katonah, a far northern suburb. It faced a loud and busy
road, and had a commercial dog kennel right behind it. The good
news, her friend explained with dark humor, is that you won't be able
to hear the dogs because of the road, or the road because of the dogs.
They laughed until they cried, and then she made a full-price offer. The
sellers responded by withdrawing the house from the market, so they
could later repost it at a higher price.

Now it was my turn. Because I was already living in New York,
I could take the second stab at finding a home. After work, I would
race north to the suburbs to meet real estate agents and look at homes.
I found a great place in Katonah that had enough room and was quite

reasonably priced. I painted pictures for Patrice with my words. They were pretty pictures. I signed a contract to buy it. She signed a contract to sell our Richmond home, and she and the kids piled into the family van and headed north. Our belongings were put into storage. The plan was to stay in my two-bedroom on John Street for a few days, then move briefly into an extended-stay hotel near our new home until we closed.

I may not have paid the attention I should have to the home I was purchasing. Yes, I know I was very busy and distracted and visited the house after dark, but still, the lights were on. Patrice and our older kids were appalled by the condition of the home. One of the kids scratched, "This is hell," on a loose slate from the front walkway. I'm pretty sure it wasn't the preschoolers, who seemed very supportive and couldn't spell that well. I had missed quite a few defects, including the fact that one of the bathrooms had no toilet, just a hole in the floor. The pre-closing inspector took Patrice aside and whispered, "Lady, can you get out of this? This is a disaster." A termite-infested main beam saved us. We got out of the contract.

We could now relax. As much as seven people living in a two-bedroom extended-stay hotel suite with no plan can relax. As much as people can relax who don't have their children enrolled in school because the school district said they would charge us seven thousand dollars per child if we didn't end up living in their school district. There was not a lot of relaxing.

The kids had a grand time. Four of them slept in one bedroom, two to a bed. The one-year-old slept in a portable crib in the kitchen, and Patrice and I slept in the other bedroom. And I got up every morning and left her, driving into Manhattan, where I, a parent whose children were not in school, was the chief federal prosecutor. Patrice would take the kids to the free hotel breakfast, and then spend the day trying to find a home, with the five kids in the car. It was a tense time in our family and our marriage. I was distracted to the point of coming apart.

One evening, we were returning to the hotel, seven of us in the van. One of the kids had a Yak Bak, a small handheld toy that could make short voice recordings and then, at the press of a button, replay the recording repeatedly. She was sitting directly behind me as I drove, bugging her siblings with the Yak Bak. I should have just let it go; we were close to the hotel. Instead, I said, in my dad voice, "Stop that."

She recorded it and started replaying my voice just behind my left ear. *"Stop that Stop that Stop that."*

I said, "You do that again and I'm throwing it out the window." She did it again, so I swiftly grabbed the toy, lowered the driver's-side window, and pitched the toy from the moving car without further comment. I raised the window and drove on, as my daughter burst into tears. "Jim!" was all Patrice said. (And, yes, I circled back to retrieve the darn thing; we weren't people who could afford to throw away perfectly good toys.)

A guiding principle to our parenting has been "always follow through on promises and threats." The kids have to know that if you say something, you mean it. It gives them a sense of security knowing they can always believe you and that, when you promise or threaten, the fences are electrified. Of course, this only works if you make thoughtful, unemotional threats.

At the end of an exhausting day, the four kids in the one bedroom wouldn't go quietly to sleep. We read books, told stories, and gave them multiple warnings. Finally, I said, "If I have to come back in here, everybody is getting whacked." They were quiet for a few minutes, then decided to see if the fence really was electrified. Furious, I burst into the dark room and hit all four, once each, with my open palm, aiming for their rears. It didn't hurt them, both because I didn't smack them hard and because they were all wearing pajama pants and under blankets, but still, it shocked them into silence for the rest of the night. It also shocked me. Patrice and I went out and sat on the floor in the hotel hallway, just outside our room door. This—a public hallway—was the only spot where we could sit, drink wine, and talk without risk of being overheard. Still, we kept our voices low. "I'm coming unglued," I whispered. "I just punished four of them without figuring out who was guilty. Collective punishment. I think it's against the Geneva Conventions. I'm losing my shit." She held my hand, smiling. "They will be fine. But we have to get out of here."

I was the leader of the most respected prosecutor's office in the nation, hitting four truant children in a dark hotel room, while a fifth slept in a Pack 'n Play against the kitchen counter, then sitting in a hotel hallway, drinking and whispering with my wife. Our kids hadn't been to school in two months. Their friends were other children at the extended-stay hotel, all of whom moved on after days or, at most, a couple of weeks. Patrice took them to nearly every museum in New York, and they had now seen every *SpongeBob SquarePants* episode. Sitting in the hallway for our nightly parents meeting, we reasoned that the museums were a form of homeschooling. *SpongeBob* was less so, although we told ourselves the show's relentless optimism and witty G-rated dialogue were good for the kids.

After eight weeks out of school, we moved to a new home—a structurally sound one Patrice found—and enrolled the kids in public schools in Somers, New York, another northern suburb. Our long nightmare was over. Of course, although it was structurally sound, the house was on a very busy road, which backed up in bumper-to-bumper traffic during rush hour. At a school event, Patrice met a woman who complimented her on the decorating choices we had made inside our home. The woman knew this because she, and hundreds of other strangers, had sat in traffic and studied the interior of our home. Curtains were a new priority. As was a new car.

The transmission on the ol' Aerostar van was shot. If Patrice paused on the upslope at the end of our driveway to check for speeding traffic before pulling out, the Aerostar would slide backward. I found a used SUV that would accommodate the seven of us, but we didn't have enough money for a down payment to the dealer, who was willing to loan us the rest at a significant interest rate. I, the United States Attorney for the Southern District of New York, asked my father to lend me five thousand dollars so I could buy a used car for my family. He agreed to lend it, but only after I signed a promissory note, with interest accruing. It bothered me to borrow money from my parents—and that a parent would demand a legal document for a five-thousand-dollar loan (with interest) from a son who was in public service and trying to get a safe car for his five grandchildren—but it bothered me more to imagine Patrice rolling backward down hills in a van full of kids. I signed the promissory note.

Almost as soon as I was officially in the U.S. Attorney job, a trial judge ruled that we had unlawfully detained a Jordanian national as part of our investigation into the terrorist attacks of September 11, 2001. She concluded that the federal statute being used to hold witnesses who might flee until they could testify before a grand jury applied only to trial witnesses. If upheld, her ruling, coming just four months after the 9/11 attacks, would gut a vital tool in the investigation. She also concluded that a New York FBI counterterrorism agent had engaged in misconduct in connection with the arrest of the witness. Both of her decisions were dead wrong, and we intended to appeal.

Main Justice made its move. The Bush administration had centralized control over terrorism investigations and prosecutions. FBI headquarters directed all FBI terror investigations, and Main Justice closely controlled prosecution decisions. New York's wings, at least when it came to terrorism cases, had at long last been clipped. They were going to send a senior Washington lawyer, likely one of Ted Olson's deputies, to argue the appeal. The ghost of Stimson moaned, although in my head his voice sounded a lot like Mary Jo's.

I returned him to the crypt by announcing that I would personally argue the appeal. If SDNY was going to maintain its culture of independence, we couldn't be just another district, where Main Justice intervened whenever it wished.

It was an unusual thing for a Justice Department leader to do. I did it only one other time, when I became deputy attorney general and argued a criminal case before the United States Supreme Court in short pants. Not shorts, but rather pants that were four inches too short. Attorneys for the government traditionally argued in the Supreme Court wearing a morning coat and striped pants, for reasons I can't explain. They had closets full of striped pants at the Department of Justice, just none with thirty-eight-inch inseams. I wore the longest pair they had, slung low, with high dark socks. Only my family, sitting behind me, noticed.

With Main Justice blocked, this time, I argued the case, wearing my own pants, and the Second Circuit Court of Appeals agreed, both on the law and the agent, reversing the trial judge. But the answer was not to have me handle every case. Without connections or wealth or a greater family, maybe I didn't have the juice to protect "our" district from Main. I might be the end of the Stimson line. Maybe that's why they picked me.

I was meeting Katie Couric at dawn to try to make it harder for Washington to push me, and my office, around. A driver shuttled me around the darkened streets, as I quickly taped interviews before 7:00 A.M. on Fox and CBS, and then headed to Rockefeller Center so I could do a "live hit" on NBC's *Today* near the beginning of the show. Next, I was off to *Good Morning America* to finish the four corners of morning news.

The NBC producer whispered that she would show me to the set where Katie and I would chat. She urged me to be very quiet because one of the show's hosts was live on air just a few yards away, across the studio. Katie would be right with me. As I crept in, I could see the brightly lit Matt Lauer looking toward me and speaking to the camera, fans on the plaza visible through the window behind him. I was very quiet and took a seat on the couch as instructed. Katie's empty armchair was to my left, a glass coffee table at my feet. At my shins, actually. When I sat down, I noticed the couch and armchair were small, and my shins were pressed against the glass table, forcing my legs wide apart. I kept hearing my mother's voice: "Were you raised in a barn?" She was a city kid who knew nothing of barns, but, for reasons now lost to time, that was her way of telling us not to sit with legs akimbo.

I was not raised in a barn. I was raised in a sixteen-hundred-square-foot suburban ranch-style house. I leaned forward to push the coffee table away from me so I could cross my legs. It moved about an inch before I noticed that the next inch would bring it crashing off the platform on which Katie's furniture rested, toward the live broadcast. I stopped pushing and, in a flash, Katie was in her chair, smiling and saying what a great case it was, and that we were live in ten seconds, and my legs were akimbo and stayed that way. My mother noticed.

So did the leadership of Main Justice. They couldn't turn on a television that morning without seeing my face. I was told they were seething, but nobody said anything to my face. So, I made more juice doing interviews and announcing big cases, and more juice visiting editorial boards, and more juice sitting for profiles in national magazines. People would say I was seeking elective office or needed the attention. Fine. But what I really needed was the profile to stay independent. Not for political ambition or vanity. For Mr. Stimson, for 1906, for the Office, to keep it away from the scent of politics. There might someday be a president who would try to corrupt the Department of Justice. The Southern District would be needed, especially, then.

CHAPTER 12

AT MAIN

*The legal judgments of the Department of Justice must be
impartial and insulated from political influence. It is imperative
that the Department's investigatory and prosecutorial powers be
exercised free from partisan consideration.*

JUSTICE DEPARTMENT MANUAL

SANDY BERGER WAS INSIDE THE NATIONAL
archives, fiddling with his sock. President Bill Clinton's former national security adviser was the only person authorized to review the most sensitive classified Clinton administration documents at America's temple to history, the enormous neoclassical building on Pennsylvania Avenue, whose architect intended to capture "the significance, security, and permanence of the records held therein." Samuel "Sandy" Berger was visiting in 2003 to help former president Clinton prepare to defend his administration's counterterrorism efforts before the 9/11 Commission, which Congress created to investigate what failings might have led to the attacks.

On this day, with the assigned Archives staff member sent off to get Berger a Diet Coke, the documents were still significant, but secure and permanent? Not so much. As the Archives staffer reported to a supervisor, "When I opened the door and started down the hall, he was stooped over right outside the doorway. He was fiddling with something white which looked to be a piece of paper or multiple pieces of paper. It appeared to be rolled around his ankle or underneath his pant leg, with a portion of the paper sticking out underneath."

Berger stole highly classified documents by stuffing them in his sock, sneaking them outside, and then, after glancing up at the windows of the Department of Justice across the street to be sure he wasn't seen, stashing them in a construction site. When he was finished reviewing materials for the evening, he left the Archives, retrieved the stashed documents, and went on his way. After the sock incident, the Archives started discreetly numbering the documents they showed Berger. Pages disappeared during other visits. When confronted, Berger lied to the investigators. Months later, he admitted he had taken five classified documents, and destroyed three; he returned the other two and his personal notes, which he had also sneaked out of the Archives building. The Department of Justice concluded he had not succeeded in depriving the 9/11 Commission of any documents; everything he stole had a backup.

I became deputy attorney general shortly after the department's Criminal Division opened an investigation into Berger's thefts. I hadn't expected to move to Washington after only two years as U.S. Attorney in New York. I knew Patrice didn't love living in the New York area—"You are going to make me die in New York" was a frequent refrain—but when I was unexpectedly asked to interview at the White House to be the deputy attorney general—the number-two position at Justice—I worried she would hesitate to uproot the kids again so soon. They now had an impressive streak of continuous school enrollment. But she was up for it immediately. "Are you kidding?

Yes. Of course. When?" For my part, I wanted to leave because the commute—routinely two hours each way—was killing me. I was regularly missing games, dinner, baths, and bedtime books. Many people in the New York legal community were puzzled that I would leave the Southern District post, even for a job that was nominally a promotion. They didn't see it as a promotion to leave the district, known as the Sovereign District, because it was the pinnacle of the profession. They didn't know the pain our living situation was causing.

We made good money on the sale of the New York house, as we rode the great American housing bubble on the way up. We used it to buy a home in northern Virginia and to pay off my father's promissory note early. The deputy attorney general job was extraordinarily difficult and stressful, but it was only eight miles from home and, for the first time, I had a driver. I was able to be present. And being the boss meant the Department of Justice would come to me, no matter where I was. I had the freedom to be with my family, as Patrice frequently reminded me, and an opportunity to model commitment to family: "If the deputy attorney general of the United States can't be at [insert name of kid activity, event, or game], who can be?" Of course, the Department of Justice needed me frequently, especially in national security cases.

In those early years after 9/11, only I and the attorney general had the authority to authorize emergency electronic surveillance under the Foreign Intelligence Surveillance Act (FISA) in terrorism cases. They didn't disturb the attorney general on nights and weekends. I had a secure phone by my bed, which Justice Department lawyers would use to call me during the night, seeking my emergency approval. But that approval started a clock. The government in those days had three days to follow it with a formal written application to the Foreign Intelligence Surveillance Court. I had to personally sign that application, which meant the department's lawyers came to me, wherever I was. The lawyers came so often to my home that the kids began to recognize them and their locked classified-materials bags, even though they had no idea what the mission was or what FISA stood for. I can close my eyes and hear the dog barking and my eight-year-old daughter shouting up the stairs, "Dad! The FISA lady is here!" The visiting attorneys—frequently women, which explains the "FISA lady" title from the kids—were talented and discreet. Too discreet, I hope, to have told anyone of the day I had to direct one of them around a large pile of dog poop in the center of the living room rug as we walked to my office to review the applications. "I'll handle that when we are done," I said, apologizing for the bracing sight.

The Sandy Berger case was one of the first I was briefed on when I took the deputy attorney general job. I shook my head. This wasn't a complicated one: the guy stole, and lied, and needed to be indicted. He had committed his crimes literally outside our windows. One year later, I was still deputy attorney general and Sandy Berger was still uncharged. I just couldn't understand it, so I asked my chief of staff to schedule weekly meetings about the case between me and Christopher Wray, the assistant attorney general for the Criminal Division, and the future FBI director after I was fired. Chris was smart, principled, and hardworking. He was also very, very, very careful. Full-stop-on-yellow-traffic-lights careful. No-swimming-for-thirty-minutes-after-eating careful.

At each weekly meeting, I pushed for explanations. The career prosecutors in Wray's division were in plea discussions and Berger's lawyer was unavailable. They wanted to double-check something with the Archives. There were classification issues they wanted to resolve before bringing charges. I mocked the excuses and said I looked forward to the new ones next week. I felt badly to be torturing Chris Wray, whom I liked very much, but the career people he supervised were dragging their feet. We needed to charge Sandy Berger even though he had powerful friends.

After a month of weekly meetings, Chuck Rosenberg, my chief of staff, spoke to me privately and told me to stop. He understood and agreed with my sense of urgency; Berger's conduct had already been widely publicized, and the lack of action from Justice undercut our credibility with the public. "But," he said, "although you don't think of yourself that way, you are a Republican political appointee pressuring your career prosecutors to charge a prominent figure from the last Democratic administration. You are going to hurt the department." Of course, that wasn't my intention, but he was right. People must never think politics influences a decision about prosecution; as the second-ranking political appointee at the department, my unusual pushing on the career prosecutors might create the impression that something political was afoot. I stopped, and never asked about the Berger case again.

In 2005, not long before I left as deputy attorney general and almost two years after Berger's thefts and lies, the Department of Justice resolved the case by letting him plead guilty to a single misdemeanor. The department recommended probation and a ten-thousand-dollar fine. The deal seemed too lenient to me. Berger stole classified top-secret, code-word-protected documents, the most sensitive stuff there is, and then lied about it. But I don't know whether the decision was wrong, because I stayed out of it. For the department.

It makes good sense that the leaders of the Department of Justice are appointed by the president, with the advice and consent of the Senate. The department has important discretion on policy questions—like what kinds of crimes to prioritize or how to approach antitrust disputes—and should be responsive in its policy choices to the will of the people, expressed through election of the president. But there is a tension in having political leaders atop the Justice Department, because the administration of justice must be evenhanded. That's why my chief of staff told me to stop pressing on the Sandy Berger case.

I love the North Carolina barrier islands. There's a spot I have visited where two islands come close together and, in the narrow gap between them, ocean water collides with the huge and shallow sound that lies behind the islands. There is turbulence in that place, and waves appear to break even though no land is visible. I have long imagined that the leaders of the Department of Justice stand at that spot, between the turbulent waters of the political world and the placid waters of the apolitical world. Their job is to respond to the political imperatives of the president and the voters who chose that president, while also protecting the apolitical work of the thousands of agents, prosecutors, and staff who make up the bulk of the institution. So long as the leaders understand the turbulence, they can find their footing. If they stumble, the ocean water overruns the sound and the department has become just another political organ. Its independent role in American life has been lost and the guardians have drowned.

Even as the deputy attorney general, responsible for supervising the department's prosecutors, I had to be careful not to focus too much on any one case with political overtones. Presidents needed to stay away entirely. And they could do that by remembering the importance of a single letter: *s*.

It is fine for political leaders to talk about cases—plural—but they should stay away from any one case—singular. The letter *s* is the difference between policy and illegitimacy. Presidents should run for office talking about the kinds of cases they expect their Department of

Justice to emphasize—environmental, or gun, or child exploitation. The American people should have a voice in the priorities of the department, through the leaders they elect. Every new president comes into office with ideas for the Department of Justice, and charges the new attorney general to carry them out. That's as it should be.

But, except in the rare case that directly implicates national security, it is never okay for a president to drop the *s* and express a view, or issue a directive, about a particular case against a particular person. By never talking about an individual criminal case, the president assures the American people that Lady Justice still has her blindfold, that decisions are being made on the facts, not politics or privilege. The difference between freedom and jail cannot be about political tribe.

George W. Bush understood. Every morning after the attacks of 9/11, he met in the Oval Office with the leaders of the FBI and the Department of Justice. We briefed him on terrorism suspects we were watching, we told him about arrests we made, we updated him on prosecutions. He never expressed a view on an individual case. He never pressed us about how we were approaching a prosecution. He listened, because the American people expected him to be up to date on the top national priority—preventing another 9/11—but he never spoke about a case. He asked about priorities—what kinds of cases were we focusing on and why? Of course, he could have pushed us on a particular case, to go hard or go easy on somebody. Nothing in the Constitution forbids it. Donald Trump, although never mistaken for a legal scholar, was most likely correct as a matter of the design of the executive branch when he claimed authority to direct the course of an individual prosecution, saying, "I'm allowed to be totally involved. I'm actually, I guess, the chief law enforcement officer of the country." As he said on another occasion, "I have absolute right to do what I want to do with the Justice Department."

George Bush surely understood that he had the power to direct the activities of the executive branch, including the Department of Justice. He had the authority to order a person prosecuted or a case dropped. He could urge the department to let someone go or lock them up. He just never did, even when I was sitting inches from him in the Oval Office, overseeing an investigation of his top advisers, a probe that was public and killing him during an election year.

People lie during investigations, for all kinds of reasons or sometimes no reason at all. That has long been true of high-level government officials. The young staffer at the Archives retrieving a Diet Coke for Sandy Berger saw him putting documents in his socks, but the former national security adviser still lied about it. It happened all the time, but a strange one landed on my desk when I became deputy attorney general.

In June 2003, a couple of months after the invasion of Iraq, an article by reporter Robert Novak had revealed the name of a covert CIA employee, despite a federal law making it a crime to identify an undercover CIA operative because the revelation might endanger the agent or her foreign sources. The revelation had come days after the CIA employee's husband had written a newspaper opinion piece attacking one of the Bush administration's main rationales for the war in Iraq—that Saddam Hussein was trying to acquire nuclear material—raising the prospect that this was some kind of political payback.

Novak said he had gotten his information from two Bush administration sources. It soon became apparent that as many as six Bush officials had spoken to reporters about the covert CIA employee. Without being asked, the deputy secretary of state contacted the Justice Department to confess he was one source. President Bush's chief

White House political adviser, Karl Rove, was apparently the second source.

But there was also evidence that a third official, Vice President Dick Cheney's chief of staff, Lewis "Scooter" Libby, spoke to numerous reporters about the CIA employee. By the time I became deputy attorney general, Libby had been interviewed by the FBI and admitted doing so, but said he only knew about the CIA employee from a reporter. He was passing gossip, not revealing classified information. A jury would conclude three years later that Libby was lying.

The law prohibiting the disclosure of the identity of a covert intelligence agent required specific and evil intent, something that would be very difficult to prove in this case, which was looking more like the reckless gossiping of senior officials.

That put the Department of Justice in a tough spot. Though the people investigating the case were professionals, I knew that it would be very difficult, if there was insufficient evidence, for a department led by Republican Attorney General John Ashcroft—for whom Rove had managed a Missouri political campaign—to credibly close an investigation against his colleagues in the same administration without recommending charges.

We had to do everything we could to protect the department's reputation for fairness and impartiality, its reservoir of trust and credibility. Ashcroft understood that, and when I met with him to discuss my recommendation that he recuse himself—step aside—from the case, he agreed. And as a high-level political appointee now myself, I couldn't supervise the case in the normal way. We needed to get it away from Main Justice, so I appointed my former colleague Patrick Fitzgerald, then serving as the United States Attorney in Chicago, as special counsel to oversee the investigation. Although Fitzgerald was a political appointee and a close friend of mine, he had a strong reputation as an independent and, as the U.S. Attorney in Chicago, was far enough away not to be seen as part of the executive branch leadership.

In December 2003, I held a press conference to announce the appointment, which was consistent with the department's practice in matters of significant public interest to confirm investigations and report their completion, even without charges. Anytime a special prosecutor is named to look into the activities of a presidential administration it is big news and, predictably, my decision was not popular at the Bush White House. Vice President Cheney, in particular, was angry about the decision and made his displeasure plain.

President Bush was different. I was with the president dozens of times during the course of that investigation, including alone with him during a tense conversation in his private dining room about NSA surveillance. He was in a tight reelection campaign and the investigation was being used by his opponent as evidence of his allegedly corrupt leadership. It was a cloud over him. Bush never mentioned the case. He never threw shade at me. It was as if it didn't exist.

The week I left office as deputy attorney general, in August 2005, Patrice and I took the five kids to the White House for a farewell Oval Office picture with President Bush. The kids thought my Justice Department job had been cool, and the little ones especially were going to miss the kindness of the deputy U.S. marshals who guarded me. My oldest daughter—then in high school—was less sad to lose them. Patrice and I confronted her one evening because we suspected she had been out without permission and with a boy we didn't trust. Using my interrogation experience, I bluffed her, saying a member of the security team had spotted her, so she shouldn't bother trying to lie about where she was. She cracked and confessed, both frustrated and impressed by their coverage. It would be fifteen years before we told her it was a bluff, a revelation that shocked all our kids, for whom the surveillance story had become legend. Yes, I couldn't mislead the American people, but this was parenting, where the rules were different.

Now, as my government career ended—or so I thought—the seven of us clustered nervously in the main West Wing hallway, just across from the Roosevelt Room, whispering because the door to "the Oval" was open. A staff member told me the president was just finishing a meeting with Karl Rove. I heard Bush's voice, speaking to Rove, who was still being investigated by the Department of Justice.

"Hey, get out of here," Bush said. "Comey's coming in, so go that way."

The smiling president emerged through the open door, ushering us into the empty Oval Office. We never saw Rove.

A decade later, when I became FBI director, Barack Obama showed that he also knew to stay away from a case. He kept the FBI director at arm's length; his White House counsel stayed in the room even when he interviewed me for the job. He warned me that we would never speak casually again once I was leading the FBI, and he kept that commitment. For my part, I knew when he was downstairs playing basketball in the FBI headquarters gym, but, despite my love for the game, I never went down.

When I got to Washington as the deputy attorney general, in late 2003, the topics I needed to speak to the public about only grew: corporate fraud, drugs, guns, terrorism, and a host of crimes associated with our growing reliance on the internet—child pornography, identity theft, computer hacking. To trust us, the American public needed to know what we were doing to protect them, and why. Among the cases that generated the most public confusion and concern during my time as deputy attorney general was President Bush's decision to have an American citizen named Jose Padilla held in military custody without trial. Padilla, a former Chicago gang member, had associated himself with the Al Qaeda terrorist organization, a group against which the Department of Justice had a long and successful record of prosecution. When I was U.S. Attorney in Manhattan, we were holding Padilla as a material witness in a terrorism investigation when the order came down from the president that he was to be handed over to the United States military, which would hold him in a military brig as an "enemy combatant." I was stunned by the directive. I had never heard of an American civilian being held without trial by the military while on American soil. But I had no reason to believe the president's order was unlawful, so I obeyed it.

I went home and told Patrice that the military had arrived and taken away an American civilian we were holding in the criminal justice system. "What?" she asked. "How is that even possible in our country?" I explained that President Bush was acting under his authority to capture the enemy during war, even if that "enemy" was an American in the United States. There was some precedent for it— President Roosevelt ordered a military trial for an American arrested in New York during World War II, and Lincoln treated some civilians as captured enemies during the Civil War—but I said I didn't fully understand what was going on. "Whoa," she said. "That's a very big deal."

She was right. For good reason, Padilla's case generated intense interest and controversy. And the controversy, and doubt about our institutions, only grew when so little information was made public about Padilla's case. Serious, thoughtful people wondered whether the case represented a fundamental and troubling move away from the rule of law in the United States. If a citizen could be jailed on the president's say-so, what are the limits to that? Doesn't this mean that none of us is safe from random military detention? Are we on a path to authoritarianism?

I was not in a position as United States Attorney to address these corrosive doubts. I didn't have access to the classified information our government had about Padilla, and the case was no longer in my jurisdiction after the military came and took him away. But when I became deputy attorney general, that all changed. As a participant in the National Security Council decision-making process, and as a senior leader of the organization now defending the military's detention of this American citizen, I had access to a lot of information.

As I read the then-classified material and learned that Padilla had admitted he met with Al Qaeda's operational leaders in Afghanistan, went through terrorist training, including specialized explosives training, and returned to America to carry out a mass attack, I realized that the American people would benefit from knowing as much of it as possible, given their legitimate interest in knowing what this unprecedented use of presidential power was all about. And it struck me that the release of the information would not jeopardize sources and methods because, although some things came from the seizure of documents—like Padilla's Afghan Al Qaeda training camp forms, with his fingerprint—much of it came from military interviews of Padilla himself.

His statements were never going to be admissible in a court of law, because he was isolated and kept from his lawyer, but they painted a credible picture of a dangerous terrorist whom the Department of Justice couldn't stop through the criminal justice system. I pressed department lawyers to see if there was any whiff that Padilla had been physically mistreated by the military; they assured me he had not been. His statements would never be accepted in an American court, but they weren't the product of torture.

There wasn't enough admissible evidence to charge him, he was a citizen who couldn't be deported, and the idea of releasing him and following him was the product of too much television; it is impossible to effectively surveil someone continuously, especially in an urban environment. With no options and a duty to protect the country, President Bush had made a good-faith decision in a highly unusual case to use military detention to save innocent lives. Maybe he was wrong, maybe he was right, but he wasn't acting on whim.

I began to push my staff to see how much of the Padilla information could be declassified. And I kept pushing, bolstered by the intense congressional interest in the case, from both Democrats and Republicans. The Department of Justice, with the agreement of the United States intelligence community, produced a detailed, unclassified summary of the information in Padilla's case. In response to the congressional interest, we sent the summary to the Senate Judiciary Committee, which promptly made it public. I then stood before cameras at the Department of Justice and recited what was in the public summary. I spoke in front of the press so the disclosure would get the attention it deserved. I wasn't trying to run for office or smear Padilla. I was trying to foster trust in the institution by telling the American people the truth about something they cared about. Transparency was essential to trust.

In Padilla's case, the American people needed to know, in a way that required details, that the case was highly unusual and didn't represent some abandonment of the rule of law. He was a really bad guy, by his own admission, bent on doing horrific things, but we had insufficient admissible evidence with which to hold him in our civilian courts. And removing him from the country he wished to attack was not an option; he was an American citizen. After the announcement, other than attacks on me, the controversy over the Padilla case subsided; the American people's trust had been protected, which was the point of the whole effort.

———

The Justice Department's tradition of revealing details about the conduct of uncharged people in cases of great public interest—the protection of the reservoir of trust through transparency—would become central to my career.

But I couldn't see that from 2004. I couldn't see that the pain in the wake of the 2014 killing of Michael Brown in Ferguson, Missouri, would lead the department to release the full record of an FBI investigation. I couldn't see that the corrosive doubts about Justice would require that we explain what we had learned about Secretary of State Hillary Clinton's conduct in 2016 and why there was no criminal case to bring against the candidate. I couldn't see how the lack of transparency around a special prosecutor's investigation of a president would mislead a country and harm the department.

I would see it all soon enough.

CHAPTER 13

THE WHOLE TRUTH

*A lack of transparency results in distrust and a deep
sense of insecurity.*
DALAI LAMA

TWENTY-SEVEN YEARS AFTER THE FLY stole the drugs
and my case agent messed with the money and my bosses required
me to tell the whole truth, I was director of the FBI. Something terrible had happened, and I needed to tell the American people.

The thin twenty-one-year-old man with bowl-cut hair slipped
through a side door, wearing a gray sweatshirt and a fanny pack.
White supremacist Dylann Storm Roof walked into the Emanuel
AME Church on Calhoun Street in Charleston on a sticky humid
June evening in 2015. He sat for an hour with a regular prayer group,
the only white participant among the traditionally African American
congregation. After the discussion of scripture, Roof stood up, pulled
a Glock 41 .45-caliber pistol from his fanny pack, starting spewing
racist hate, and began killing the church members. Roof reloaded
that new Glock five times as he slaughtered nine good people. He told
one woman he was going to spare her so she could tell others what he

had done and why. He walked out of the church and was captured three days later, after a massive police and FBI manhunt.

Two weeks later, on Thursday, July 9, I had my regular quarterly meeting with the reporters who covered the FBI. It was called a "pen and pad" because no photographs or broadcast recording were allowed, with the hope that it would foster a more substantive exchange if I sat, without a jacket, and just answered questions on the record. We held it every three months in the director's dining room at FBI headquarters, a space that was apparently intended during construction in the early 1970s to offer J. Edgar Hoover a grand venue for meals, complete with a full chef's kitchen. But Hoover died before the building was finished. I tended to eat sandwiches at my desk. Still, it was a good space to host foreign visitors and to talk with the media.

The purpose of these gatherings was to try to offer Americans, through the media, a detailed picture—or as much of one as possible—of the FBI's work. The July 9 session was typical and covered a wide range of topics, with a special focus on the so-called Islamic State, the terror group that had seized territory in Syria and Iraq and was using it to urge Americans to engage in acts of violence at home, or travel to the "caliphate." None of the reporters crowded around the huge rectangular dining table draped in a blue cloth asked about the Emanuel AME killer; he had already been captured and the prosecution was under way.

After the pen and pad, I went through the rest of my day, which included a late-afternoon meeting with Amy Hess, the career special agent who led the FBI's Science and Technology Branch. STB included our enormous facility in West Virginia that administered the federal background-check system for firearms. Millions of times each year, FBI employees took information from gun dealers and researched the background of someone who wanted to buy a gun. These were some of the hardest-working people in the FBI, their workload swollen by huge spikes in gun purchases by people concerned the Obama administration was coming for their guns.

Executive Assistant Director Hess wanted to see me to tell me something she had learned about the Roof case. Hess was a tall, fit fifty-year-old who still had the bearing of the astronaut she had planned to be after getting her astronautical and aeronautical engineering degree from Purdue. The FBI recruited her in graduate school and, although she never went into space, she had risen to become one of our stars. She looked at me across the corner of the conference table. "We made a mistake. Dylann Roof should not have been able to buy the gun he used to kill those poor people in Charleston."

As was typical in the FBI when terrible news was delivered, I kept my gaze steady and simply said, "Say more." And she did. Roof had been arrested for drug possession shortly before he tried to buy the Glock 41. Through an accident of South Carolina's geography, and a gap in our protocols, the examiner who took the call about Roof's intended purchase checked with the wrong police departments to see if they had any information that Roof had been convicted or that he was a user of illegal drugs. If the examiner had checked in the right place, the records would have shown Roof admitted to the arresting officers that he was a drug user. That would have led to a quick denial of the purchase. Instead, Roof got the gun. And killed nine innocent people because they were Black. I felt ill.

As I listened to Amy Hess, I saw three things quickly: first, the Bureau needed to make a public statement about this, immediately; second, we needed to tell the victims' families; and third, I needed to make sure the examiner who made this understandable mistake was okay. I instructed our public affairs people to assemble the press corps again in the morning, and I asked for the phone number of the West Virginia employee.

The next morning, I had an emotional private call with the fire-arms background-check examiner, who was in a great deal of pain. I confirmed that our people in Charleston were already meeting with the families. Then I walked into the dining room and sat before the reporters, in the same chair as the previous day. As I looked around the table at them, crammed together with tented paper name cards arrayed like two zippers down the table, I felt a wave of emotion hit me. It startled me. I paused, took a deep breath, and then told them the truth. That all of us at the Bureau were sick that this had happened. We wished we could turn back time, but we couldn't.

Like the Department of Justice of which it is a part, the FBI depends upon the trust and confidence of the American people. If the FBI isn't trusted—in courtrooms, on street corners, and at cookouts—it can't keep people safe. And being trusted means telling the truth, about successes and failures. We had failed, and we owed the country—and the victims—the truth, a concept at the heart of the institution. The American people could decide what to do with that truth, but they had to know it, all of it.

I never planned to be in the director's dining room because I was never going to be FBI director. When Robert Mueller was approaching the end of his ten-year term, in 2011, he told me I should be the next director. I said no. Someone from the White House counsel's office reached out to a friend of mine to ask if I was interested. After checking with me, my friend passed back my answer: "No." I wasn't ready to go back to government, especially for that high-stress job. After leaving the Department of Justice in 2005, I had been diagnosed with cancer and endured a brutal course of radiation, surgery, and chemotherapy, which left me with lasting physical problems, including that my feet and fingertips were permanently numb. The legacy of cancer would make being FBI director more challenging. My colleagues at the Connecticut-based investment firm Bridgewater Associates, where I was serving as general counsel, designed an elaborate April Fool's joke to pretend that the president was trying to reach me to pressure me about the FBI position. It was pretty clever, but I didn't take the call. I wanted the idea to go away. And it did, when Congress extended Mueller's term for another two years.

Two years later, it came back, with a call from the attorney general, asking me to interview for the job. With Patrice's encouragement, I agreed to visit Washington. Not long after, President Obama announced that I would replace Bob Mueller. I moved to Washington without Patrice and the kids and came home as often as I could on weekends. They would follow me in two years, when it made sense for their schooling. Which was just as well, because I had a lot to do; there were some issues.

People had been executed after trials where FBI lab examiners gave erroneous testimony. People were serving decades in prison all over America after the FBI lab exaggerated the significance of hair comparisons. I was shocked to learn about it when I became FBI director.

Hair is not like fingerprints. Its shape and color cannot be used as a form of identification. Until DNA analysis of hair became possible, the science of hair comparison could only narrow the possible source of a hair to a group of unknown size, not to an individual. That's because nobody has done the work to figure out whether the hairs from two different humans ever look identical under a microscope. For that reason, hair can be used to exclude a suspect—"that couldn't be one of his hairs because it looks totally different"—but it can't be used to establish guilt. The most an examiner could say is that a hair found at a crime scene is "consistent with the defendant's hair, but we don't know how many other people have hairs that also look like the hair found at the scene." In other words, it could have come from the defendant, but it could have come from someone else. At best, it was marginal proof.

But over decades, beginning at least as early as the 1970s and continuing until the late 1990s—when DNA analysis became part of hair comparison—the way the FBI's witnesses described hair evidence drifted, and got much stronger than the science. Without standards in place to tell them what they could and couldn't say, and in a lab environment of overconfidence—even arrogance—witnesses from the FBI lab started suggesting to juries that it was a form of identification. They frequently wrote reports that said a crime scene hair was "consistent with having come from the defendant's head." That was bad, but in courtroom testimony, it almost always got worse. Sometimes they told juries that, in thousands of cases, they had never encountered a situation in the lab where two people had hair that looked identical under a microscope. Sometimes they went a bit further and said that, in their opinion, the hair found at the crime scene was likely, or probably, or almost definitely, the defendant's. And sometimes they went all the way into blatant scientific falsehood, telling the jury the hair found on the victim's sweater came from the defendant's head.

The FBI people weren't lying. They believed what they said about their work. They were well-meaning. It was still all wrong. None of those assertions were supported by science. But nobody in the courtroom knew that. Scientists from the FBI said it, prosecutors argued it, and juries believed it. In thousands of cases, in federal and state courts all over the country, in the 1970s, '80s, and '90s. It was a catastrophe. Maybe most of those defendants were guilty and the FBI proof was unimportant. Maybe. But surely some of them were innocent and the FBI proof was crucial. And some of these people might still be in jail, or might have been executed, or were about to be.

Some of them were undoubtedly innocent and the bad hair testimony had convicted them. Starting in 2009, several defendants in the District of Columbia were exonerated by DNA for violent-crime convictions in which FBI lab employees had testified about matching hair. *The Washington Post* wrote about those cases, pushing the FBI into action.

In 2012, director Robert Mueller reached a private agreement with defense organizations—the Innocence Project and the National Association of Criminal Defense Lawyers—to accelerate and systematize the review of all prior hair-comparison testimony, prioritizing death penalty cases where the defendant had not yet been executed. When I became director a year later and was told about the problem and the process, it was under way. The project was massive, involving the review of thousands of old files and an effort to recover trial transcripts to see what the FBI people had told juries. By 2015, it was clear we had a huge problem.

As of March 2015, we had reviewed about 500 of the 3,000 cases involving hair comparison. In the 268 cases where examiners provided testimony used to convict a defendant at trial, 257 (96 percent) had bad testimony. Errors were identified in 33 of the 35 cases that resulted in a sentence of death. Nine of those defendants had already been executed and five died of other causes while on death row. FBI examiners had testified in 41 states, and nearly all of them made errors in the way they described the hair comparison.

It was awful. The public really had no idea how bad our work had been. I decided it made sense to tell them, so we issued joint press statements with the defense organizations working with us on the project. My purpose wasn't to hurt the FBI; it was to force the FBI to stare at and fix its problems, and force state authorities to remedy injustice. I also wanted to lock in the size of the problem, so there could be no going back. Because I know how it is with mistakes in the criminal justice system.

People say inspiring things about their commitment to justice, but it is really hard to get humans to admit mistakes in pursuit of that commitment. A big part of that reluctance is that injustice is often an abstraction. When I got word that people at the lab were unhappy with how I was handling the hair controversy, I went down to have lunch with a group of them. None of these scientists had been involved with hair examinations, but the lab was their life. Over sandwiches, they shared important concerns: they were worried about the lab, its reputation and morale. They had worked for two decades to fix the lab, professionalize it, attract great scientists, and produce consistent, defendable work. This publicity was going to damage all that. They were also worried that the defense organizations with which we had partnered had a hidden agenda—to delegitimize all lab comparisons except DNA, to kill off analysis of paint, fibers, tires, bullets, hand-writing, voice patterns, and so much more that played a role in our investigations.

Maybe so, I replied, but we gave bad testimony in hundreds of cases and innocent people might be in jail all over this country because of us. We needed to fix that, and all the consequences to the FBI were secondary. They all nodded and said they agreed, but I left with the sense that, even to these good, smart people, the abstraction of hundreds of innocent people lacked power. The hundreds weren't in the room. Maybe if a convicted innocent person had been there, even if the case didn't involve hair evidence, it would feel different. Maybe if they remembered Jeff Cox, the way I did.

Cox just sat there staring. His eyes were dead. Most people serving life in prison after all appeals are done either angrily protest their innocence or admit their crimes. Jeff Cox did neither; he just sagged. An FBI agent was at the state prison because he was investigating a series of knife murders in central Virginia that appeared to be the work of a serial killer. Cox had been convicted in the brutal knife killing of an elderly woman in Richmond. There had been two men involved in the kidnapping and murder, according to witnesses, but only Cox was caught. Maybe he was a lead to the serial killer, or maybe he was the killer himself, so the agent went up the James River to the state pen. Dead-eyed, Cox explained that he couldn't help the agent because he hadn't been involved in the crime. If he had been, he would tell the agent, because he had nothing to lose, but he had lost everything for something he didn't do and had nothing left to give. The encounter left the agent shaken. He had interviewed hundreds of prisoners and never walked out of a jail with the sense that something was terribly wrong. He couldn't sleep. He kept seeing Cox and his dead eyes.

The crime had been savage. In 1990, in Richmond, an elderly woman named Ilouise Cooper was dragged from her home in the middle of the night by a knife-wielding man, who pulled her from the house as her invalid husband screamed for help. This guy pushed her into a waiting car driven by another man and they drove away. There were two eyewitnesses, one a single mother living next door and the other a man on the street. The next day, Mrs. Cooper was found, stabbed to death, in a park not far away.

The community was outraged by the crime, and a team of Richmond police officers, led by an experienced, even legendary, homicide detective, began the hunt for her killer. They got a tip that the killing had been an act of revenge by drug purchasers who had been ripped off by a drug dealer who lived on the same block as Ilouise Cooper. They developed the theory (which later turned out to be correct) that Mrs. Cooper had been murdered by mistake, when the killers went to the wrong address and concluded she must be the drug dealer's mother or grandmother and her life would be payment for the rip-off. An informant gave them the name of a suspect and they started investigating that suspect, who was well known to the authorities. As they did so, they came to learn the suspect had an acquaintance named Jeff Cox, who resembled a sketch of the assailant who dragged Mrs. Cooper from her home. The sketch had been done by a police artist from one eyewitness's description.

The investigating team took photos of Cox, who had no criminal record and a regular job as an air-conditioning repairman, and showed them to the two eyewitnesses. The police kept no record of the photo identification procedure, other than to note that the witnesses positively identified Cox.

Cox was arrested and charged with first-degree murder. The prosecution had no weapon, no forensics, and no motive evidence. The prosecutor's trial file was a nearly empty single manila folder. Cox hired a lawyer, who tried Cox's case during a two-day break in a death penalty case he was in the middle of trying, and did little investigation. In a trial that lasted less than two days, the prosecution called the two eyewitnesses, Cox offered a girlfriend as his alibi, and the jury convicted him in short order. He was sentenced to life in prison.

Nearly ten years later, I came to know this case because the FBI agent who couldn't sleep brought it to the U.S. Attorney's Office in Richmond, where I was the supervisor. He was convinced an innocent man was in jail for life. He convinced us to support an investigation, and we opened one on the flimsy basis that it was a drug-related killing where everybody agreed at least one perpetrator was at large.

Working with the FBI, Assistant U.S. Attorney Bob Trono then proved, beyond a shadow of a doubt, that Cox was innocent, and developed powerful evidence implicating two others. He found the drug dealer involved in the initial dispute, the one whose "grandmother" the killers wrongly thought Mrs. Cooper was. The dealer didn't know Cox and identified two other guys as the people he was fighting. One of those guys drove a car that matched the kidnappers' and worked as a chef with a collection of specialized knives, one of which matched the stab wounds in Mrs. Cooper. The chef's ex-wife saw him the day after the killing, his shoulder covered in scratches that he explained came from some "bitch." And, finally, when confronted with this evidence in an interview with his lawyer present, the chef admitted he participated in the abduction and murder with an associate of his, the same guy the drug dealer identified.

With the new evidence, we discussed the case with the police and the local prosecutor. The police officers were outraged that we were spending federal resources to help this guy who was clearly guilty of killing an elderly woman. The eyewitnesses, one of whom I interviewed, were similarly outraged that we were suggesting they got it wrong. The prosecutor's reaction was odd; he said he thought at the time of trial that Cox was guilty, but was always troubled by the fact that he went to jail for life without trying to cooperate, which had been the prosecutor's hope all along. But, whatever his concerns, he decided it was up to a jury to resolve any doubts about the case.

It took a dark turn when the FBI agent assigned to the case became convinced a detective on the murder of Ilouise Cooper was corrupt and had intentionally framed Cox, and the agent started following the detective around. I asked him to please hold off on investigating the cop because we needed his support to untangle the

Cox case. He refused and said he could help free Cox and investigate the detective at the same time. I went to the FBI to meet with the leaders of the Richmond division. For the only time in my career, I asked them to remove an agent from a case. I explained that our mission now was to free an innocent man from a life in prison and, we hoped, find a murderer who had escaped justice. Police corruption was important, and I had no view on whether the police detective was corrupt—although I had seen no evidence—but we had convinced him to help us and I wouldn't allow that to be jeopardized by the FBI agent's behavior. The agent was removed, and hated me for it.

The Commonwealth of Virginia told us it was not going to free Jeff Cox unless we established that someone else was guilty in a way that precluded Cox's guilt. Although state officials privately agreed that Cox appeared to be innocent, the governor was not going to free a high-profile defendant—in a case without a DNA exoneration because there was no DNA evidence—unless he could show the public we got the real killer, despite extraordinary pressure in the form of editorials about the case by *The Washington Post*.

To free Cox, Trono was sent to Virginia state court to work temporarily as a local prosecutor. He indicted, tried, and convicted the chef for being one of the two participants; the evidence included a statement by this new defendant in which he admitted driving the car and identified the other guy who dragged Ilouise Cooper from her apartment. When a guilty man was indicted, Cox was freed, after serving eleven years for a crime he didn't commit. The second man was never charged because the chef refused to testify against him.

Abstractions don't stare at you. They don't have dead eyes. And nobody gets promoted by messing with cases that are finished. We issued the press statements about hair-comparison errors to tell the world how big a problem the FBI had caused. I met with the FBI employees assigned to the review of old cases to praise them and support them. I told them I would be carefully following their work, as they pushed through hundreds of files. I promised them I would help them, and wrote letters to dozens of governors pleading for their help in finding old trial transcripts and urging them to review the work of their state lab examiners, whom the FBI had trained for forty years. "We want to make sure there aren't other innocent people in jail because of our work," I wrote. "Like you, we care deeply about justice, which is both about obtaining convictions and making sure mistakes are fixed. I am very sorry the FBI put you in this position and am grateful for your help."

In admitting the mistakes with hair comparison, we were, of course, trying to remedy injustice in individual cases. But by admitting our mistakes publicly, we were trying to do something larger. If the American people were to trust us, they needed to know we would speak the truth, including about ourselves. Maybe especially about ourselves. They needed to believe us when we said we saw something, when we made a promise, or when we corrected a mistake. They needed to know we were not part of any political tribe, that we were interested only in finding truth. Without the trust of our fellow citizens, we were ineffective. That trust would be put to the test at doorways all around Ferguson, Missouri.

At noon on Saturday, August 9, 2014, Michael Brown lay dead in the middle of Canfield Drive in Ferguson, shot by police officer Darren Wilson. For a few awful minutes, the street and the community were still, and then the neighborhood, and the country, came apart. It was quiet at first, as investigators worked the crime scene, leaving the victim's body in place—the common police procedure—to capture evidence and take measurements. But in the twenty minutes before Brown's body was covered with a sheet, local residents gathered at the site, some shouting death threats at the officers. The anger built. Crime scene work was twice stopped after reports of gunfire in the area. A candlelight vigil the next day was followed by looting and fires, kicking off nights of unrest.

As is typical, the primary responsibility for examining the circumstances of the killing of Michael Brown was with the local authorities, and the St. Louis County prosecutor began his own investigation. But on Monday, August 11, we at the FBI decided to open our own federal civil rights investigation into Brown's death. Things were too tense, and the gulf between the Black community and local law enforcement too large, for us not to promise we would take a separate look at this.

That same day, two men who said they saw the shooting told reporters that Brown had his hands raised in surrender when the officer fired repeatedly. Given the broken relationship between Ferguson's police and its Black citizens—the product of an oppressive and racist law enforcement and municipal culture—the killing of an eighteen-year-old unarmed Black man by a white police officer would have been deeply troubling in any context. The accounts about a surrendering Brown being executed—which turned out to be false—were gasoline on the fire.

That night, police in riot gear fired tear gas and rubber bullets to try to disperse a crowd of protesters in Ferguson. Images from the protests showed many officers equipped with military-style gear, including armored vehicles, body armor, and assault rifles. In photos circulated online, officers were seen pointing their weapons at demonstrators.

Three days later, local authorities released surveillance video showing Michael Brown shoving a Ferguson Market clerk and stealing cigarillos minutes before he was shot dead by the police officer. Release of the video enraged protesters, who saw it not as transparency but as an effort to defame the dead young man. Missouri's governor imposed a curfew and deployed the National Guard. Unrest lasted for many days.

Things grew quieter in Ferguson until three days before Thanksgiving, when the county prosecutor announced that a state grand jury had decided not to indict the officer. Protests that evening again turned violent. At least a dozen buildings and multiple police cars were burned, officers were hit by rocks and batteries, and gunfire echoed around St. Louis.

In the middle of all that pain and tumult after Michael Brown was killed, the FBI was trying to figure out on our own what had happened. We sent dozens of agents into the community to knock on doors and ask questions. In pairs, these men and women approached hundreds of doorways. As they knocked, they were wearing business dress, with unbuttoned blue raid jackets bearing the agency's initials in big yellow letters. There could be no doubt who they worked for. And a remarkable thing happened. Every door opened and people spoke to us. Hundreds of people, at more than three hundred homes, answered our questions, telling us what they had seen, what they knew, and who else we should interview. A community that despised its police department trusted the strangers from the FBI.

Agents combined the results of that canvass and interviews with more than one hundred people who said they had been eyewitnesses and, working with the Department of Justice's Civil Rights Division, analyzed physical, ballistic, forensic, and crime scene evidence; medical and autopsy reports; audio and video recordings; and cell phone and social media data. After all that work, it was apparent that the evidence didn't show what most people, based on media accounts, expected it to show.

The Department of Justice Civil Rights Division also conducted a parallel "pattern and practice" review of the Ferguson Police Department, which took longer than the criminal investigation and found an appalling, yearslong pattern of abuse of the Black community and a municipal culture in which African Americans were targeted as a key source of town funding—through the tickets and fines imposed on them by the overwhelmingly white police department.

With both the criminal and pattern-and-practice investigations completed, the department showed our work to the American people, issuing two reports on the same day—one was 83 pages on the criminal investigation and the second 102 pages about the culture and practice of the Ferguson police. We were not bringing charges, but as it has long done in cases of intense and legitimate public interest, the department described what investigation we did, what we learned, and what conclusions we drew. Announcing the result alone wasn't meaningful transparency; people—especially people who had been given bad information for months—deserved the details; they needed them, if they were going to trust that justice was being done.

The evidence was not adequate to charge Officer Wilson with a crime. The proof showed that Wilson was driving in his department-issued marked SUV when he saw Michael Brown and his friend walking in the middle of Canfield Drive. The two young men had just come from the Ferguson Market, where surveillance video showed Brown stealing several packages of cigarillos and then, when the store clerk tried to stop him, using his large size to stand over the clerk and forcefully shove him away. A witness heard Brown say to the clerk, as he shoved, "What you gonna do?" In his vehicle, Wilson's radio received the Ferguson Police dispatch of a "stealing in progress" at the nearby store, including a description of Brown and his friend.

When Wilson came upon two men fitting the radioed description, walking in the middle of the road, he ordered them to walk on the sidewalk, and called for backup, radioing, "Put me on Canfield with two and send me another car." Brown's friend testified that Wilson told them to "get the fuck on the sidewalk." Wilson had already driven past the two men, so he backed his SUV and parked at an angle, blocking the road and their path. As Officer Wilson attempted to open his car door, the door was blocked by Brown's body and closed abruptly, with Wilson still in the car. The officer maintained that Brown said, "What the fuck are you gonna do?" before slamming the door shut. Brown's friend said the door opened quickly as they neared the car and bounced off Brown, causing it to slam shut.

Regardless, credible witnesses and physical evidence established what happened next: Michael Brown reached in the police vehicle and began hitting the smaller Wilson in the face and upper body, bruising the officer's face and scratching his neck. The two grappled as Wilson tried to block the blows. Unable to reach any of his other police weapons while seated and fighting with Brown, Wilson began to withdraw his gun from the holster on his right hip. Brown reached across the officer to grab the gun and the two struggled over it. Wilson fired one round, striking Brown in the hand at close range. DNA evidence inside the car, on Wilson's shirt collar, and on the gun, and analysis of the wound to Brown's hand, confirmed Wilson's account that Brown leaned inside the car and grabbed for the gun when it fired.

Wounded in the hand, Brown began to run away down Canfield

Drive. Wilson got out of the car and began chasing him, gun in hand. All the credible witnesses, and the ballistics and autopsy reports, established that Wilson did not fire until Brown stopped, turned, apparently took a small hop, and then began charging back at the officer. The evidence showed that Wilson fired three volleys as Brown closed the distance, for a total of ten shots. As he moved toward the officer, Brown was hit multiple times, finally dying instantly when the last shot hit the top of his head as he leaned forward several feet from Wilson. Brown lay dead on his stomach, with one hand balled up at his waistband and the injured hand by his side.

Although several people claimed to have seen Brown with hands up surrendering, investigators could not reconcile those claims with the physical evidence, prior statements by the alleged witnesses, and credible witnesses. Some who told the media they had seen Brown shot with hands up admitted they had not seen the shooting at all. Although credible witnesses gave varying accounts of what Brown was doing with his hands as he moved toward Wilson—balling them, holding them out, or pulling up his pants—and different accounts of his movement—charging, "slow motion," or running—they all confirmed that Brown was moving toward the officer when he was shot. Even those witnesses who recalled that Brown briefly held his hands palms-out at shoulder level told investigators Brown dropped his hands and charged at Wilson before being shot.

This was a tragedy on many levels. A young man lost his life. An oppressed community exploded. An officer's life was forever marked. But the Department of Justice, by offering a comprehensive report on the death of Michael Brown and the racism of Ferguson, made an important difference. For those who wanted the truth—what happened both on Canfield Drive and for years in Ferguson before that awful day—there were facts, laid out in great detail. The people of

Ferguson trusted us, and we repaid the trust by telling the truth. The reservoir made a difference. It didn't fix our country, which had—and still has—a long way to go on race and policing, but, in one place, Ferguson, Missouri, the reservoir contributed to change—of the police, the political leadership, and the community.

PART FOUR

Draining the Reservoir

In a savagely partisan election year, I learned that truth and transparency aren't always enough to safeguard the Justice Department's credibility when the attacks come from all sides. And then I watched as the Trump administration did significant additional damage to the reservoir of trust. Violations of the traditions of nonpartisan law enforcement and constant presidential attacks on the institution, aided and abetted by an attorney general who abused his role, depleted trust in the Justice Department in a way that hadn't happened since Watergate. Each lie, each act of favoritism toward friends and retaliation against enemies, each demonstration that the department was loyal to the president alone, brought water gushing out. The damage has been grave, but history shows the way back. Justice can be saved.

CHAPTER 14

SHIT SHOW

Everyone is entitled to his own opinion, but not to his own facts.
DANIEL PATRICK MOYNIHAN

THE FBI WANTED NO PART OF the 2016 presidential election, a battle between the two least-trusted candidates in the history of modern polling. But we were thrust into it by a criminal referral from the intelligence community inspector general over Hillary Clinton's mishandling of classified information on her private email system. Of course, the partisans all knew the answer before we even started our investigation. According to the Clinton camp, it wasn't even an investigation, but a mere "review" that would show no wrongdoing. From the Trump side came the "lock her up" chant, for what they shouted was a horrific national security breach. My Sunday-school teacher wife called it "a shit show." Although I never repeated her description at work, she was right: we were trying to find truth in an environment where few political figures cared what was true; they just wanted to win. The FBI would not get out of this without damage.

———

My work life was stressful, but after two years, Patrice and I were reunited and living in the D.C. area with our youngest daughter, who was still in high school. Being able to see my family every day lightened the load. And they had grown accustomed to the job, especially the security team of FBI special agents who protected me. Only some of it still seemed bizarre—like my teaching our high schooler to drive on the roads of the FBI's Quantico training academy. But otherwise the presence of armed agents at family outings, weddings, and vacations was normal. Each year, Patrice bought a catered Thanksgiving meal for the team, and they thanked her with an annual photo of themselves in suits and sunglasses around a table, fearsome weapons visible. The pictures are still on our shelves at home, framed.

Despite their comfort with the people on my security team, the younger kids were still mortified when I played music from Taylor Swift or One Direction on my iPhone speaker as we traveled in an armored vehicle behind stone-faced agents. Like true professionals, the detail members never showed that they were listening, but, like true professionals, they were. That's how the team leader knew our youngest was a huge fan of the author John Green, who was the speaker at our son's college graduation. That's why, upon seeing Mr. Green after the graduation about to get into a parked car outside the university venue, the detail leader, riding in the front passenger seat, abruptly held up his left fist, signaling an immediate halt to our motorcade, which screeched to a stop and blocked Mr. Green's car, as the agent leapt from the vehicle. "Sir, sir," he called out, using his best executive cadence, "could you wait just a moment?" He then swept open the rear door of the black Suburban, looked at our youngest, and said, "Now's your chance. We got 'im." Mortified and thrilled, our daughter climbed from the car and met the talented—and barricaded—Mr. Green, still in his academic regalia. The FBI director got out and took a picture of them together. Then the FBI released John Green, who had been very gracious and seemed to find the whole thing amusing. We would all need to find reasons to smile as we steamed into 2016.

By early 2016, it was starting to look like we did not have a prosecutable case against Hillary Clinton. If the investigation continued on the same trajectory, the challenge was going to be closing the case in a way that maintained the confidence of the American people that their Justice Department was working in an honest, competent, and nonpolitical manner. The reservoir would be at great risk as powerful political people, for whom truth is not a central value, attacked our work.

There was no doubt that, as secretary of state, Hillary Clinton had talked about secret stuff on an email system that wasn't approved for that, so the heart of the investigation was the question of Secretary Clinton's intent: Did she know she was breaking the rules, or was it some kind of sloppiness? If we couldn't prove bad intent, there was no prosecutable case. That was clear. The challenge would be convincing a polarized America that we made a credible decision, based on the facts alone.

And then President Obama increased the risk to our credibility. He spoke about the case—singular—dropping the *s* that has long kept politics out of law enforcement. Obama told *60 Minutes* on October 11, 2015, that Clinton's email use was "a mistake" that had not endangered national security, and said on Fox News on April 10, 2016, that she might have been careless but did not do anything to intentionally harm national security. We were investigating one of the two presumptive candidates for president. Secretary Clinton was a Democrat, as were the president and the attorney general. It was going to be hard enough to convince the American people the investigation was done in a nonpolitical way. President Obama made it much harder.

If the president had already decided there was no case, how could his Department of Justice reach a judgment the American people could trust? The truth was that the president had no inside knowledge about the investigation. But his comments still set all of us up for corrosive attacks if the case were completed with no charges brought.

Obama seemed to realize what he had done. After the spring of 2016, whenever a meeting or conversation involving the FBI or Justice Department leaders got near a particular case, he would volunteer a long preamble about his lack of interest in an individual case and notify all present that he wasn't commenting on a case or interested in the details of any case. But it was too late. His public prejudgment of the Clinton case was used by political opponents to accuse us of being corrupt even before the work was finished.

Attorney General Loretta Lynch made it harder still by meeting privately on a government jet with Hillary Clinton's husband, former president Bill Clinton, on June 27, 2016, just days before we finished our investigation, and then refusing to step away from the case, despite public furor. Instead, she announced she would accept my recommendation and that of the career prosecutors. Thinking of the reservoir and the transparency that helped protect it in Ferguson, and the Padilla case, and the Charleston church massacre, I stepped away from the attorney general to do something I never could have imagined before 2016: have the FBI separately offer its views to the American people, by making public my recommendation and the thinking behind it. Even in hindsight, I believe it was the best thing for the FBI and for the Department of Justice. The American people needed and deserved transparency, if they were to trust the work.

With the announcement that we were not recommending prosecution of Secretary Clinton, I thought we were done with the 2016 election and I was back to focusing full-time on recruiting diverse talent, finding good leaders, helping improve policing in the United States, cyber threats, terrorism, violent crime against children, and all the other responsibilities of the FBI. But it was not to be, because the shit show was only getting started. Three weeks later, we were compelled to start an investigation into whether any Americans associated with the Trump campaign were coordinating with the ongoing Russian election interference. It was an investigation that simply had to be opened—notwithstanding Attorney General William Barr's later repeated efforts to smear the FBI—after we received, as Special Counsel Robert Mueller wrote, "evidence that the Russians had signaled to a Trump campaign adviser that they could assist the campaign through the anonymous release of information damaging to the Democratic candidate."

Unlike the Clinton case, which had come to us publicly and which we had discussed only after it was completed—or so we thought—the new Russia investigation was classified and just beginning in the summer of 2016. We smelled smoke about the Trump campaign and Russia, but we didn't know whether there was fire. So we set out to see what we could learn, very carefully so as not to blow the investigation or smear innocent people. There were no leaks, and the work was done professionally and without political bias, as independent investigators would later find—despite some Trump-world wackiness about how we were engaged in a "deep state" effort to stop his election, with an investigation that we kept completely secret until long after he was in office.

In late October 2016, the team handling the FBI's investigation into Russian interference in the presidential election decided to seek a court order to conduct electronic surveillance of Carter Page, a former adviser to the Trump campaign. We had evidence that the Russians were looking to funnel information to the campaign. Page was one of four Americans being investigated, based on their historical connections to Russia, to see if they were the conduit. Given the information they had gathered, Page was the only one for whom investigators wanted to seek a surveillance order.

National security wiretaps—obtained under FISA, the Foreign Intelligence Surveillance Act—are different from those in criminal cases and cry out for strong oversight because they are classified and unlikely to ever be known to the target or the public. FISA was passed by Congress after Watergate—the last time the Department of Justice needed saving—and created a special court to oversee the use of electronic surveillance in national security investigations; before then, the executive branch had decided on its own when to wiretap Americans in spy or terrorism cases, a setup ripe for abuse. By the time I became FBI director, prodded by the periodic discovery of mistakes, the Department of Justice and the FBI had built a powerful oversight regime for FISA wiretaps in cases involving investigations of foreign intelligence agents, spies, and terrorists. Or at least I thought so.

The FISA applications sat each morning in a pile on the corner of my glass-covered FBI director's desk. Unlike criminal-case wiretap applications, I had to sign these myself. The stack sat directly over Hoover's 1963 memo to Bobby Kennedy about wiretapping King. The contrast between the thick modern applications to federal judges and the threadbare Hoover memo was striking and inspiring; we had come so far in constraining our own power.

Each application was accompanied by a memo showing the many sets of eyes that had reviewed the document before it got to me, all reviewers having signed to prove they had checked it. After I signed—certifying, as required by law, that a significant purpose of the application was the collection of foreign intelligence and that we had tried less-intrusive investigative techniques—the documents were headed to the Department of Justice leadership for signature and then to a federal judge on the Foreign Intelligence Surveillance Court. Between ten and twenty people personally reviewed each application.

I took additional comfort from the grousing. As I visited offices around the country, agents frequently complained that it was far harder to get a court order to read a Russian spy's emails than to listen to the Gambino crime family leadership talk over Phil Collins music. I liked that, because complaints meant the many layers of oversight and review—more than in a criminal case—were operating as designed, to check and double-check what we said in cases that would likely never see the light of day, that would never be subject to attack by a defense lawyer or scrutiny by a trial judge in a public prosecution.

The FBI had significant evidence of Carter Page's association with Russia and historical contacts with Russian intelligence. And there was very recent information from a reliable former FBI source who had privately compiled reports drawn from his own network of Russian sources—the so-called Steele dossier. FBI reviewers had different opinions as to whether the Steele information was needed to meet the legal requirement of probable cause—my general counsel thought the application was adequate even without it—but all agreed that, with both the historical information and the Steele reports, the application was appropriate. After going through the many layers of review—I read it and signed the certification—the application was presented in secret to a federal judge, who approved the surveillance for ninety days. Nobody outside the Department of Justice knew about the surveillance, which was extended by new applications and court orders three times, including after I was fired.

After the fact of the secret Page surveillance later became public—an inexcusable leak that harmed an American citizen—it formed the centerpiece of allegations by President Trump and his supporters that the FBI had engaged in a politically motivated plot to prevent his election. Even Trump's second attorney general, Bill Barr, took up the attack, muttering in public about the FBI having "spied" on the Trump campaign and hinting darkly about disturbing FBI behavior. Setting aside the unusually poor logic of alleging an FBI plot to defeat Trump after we had both kept secret that we were investigating people associated with his campaign and made disclosures close to the election that many Democrats blamed for Hillary Clinton's defeat, the allegations were absurd. The FBI's people are human, but we conducted the investigation for sound reasons, and did it without regard to politics. I was pleased when the Department of Justice inspector general announced that he would investigate the allegations of political bias at the FBI. I knew what he would find.

And I was right. When he finally finished his work, long after I was fired, the inspector general concluded that the FBI's investigation into whether any Trump associates were working with the Russians was properly opened and conducted without evidence of bias. It was a complete vindication after years of lying about the FBI by the president and his echo chamber. None of us were going to jail, despite what Trump and Fox News personalities spent two years telling viewers. The inspector general found that we did the jobs our country hired us to do.

Except I was also wrong. Although he found no evidence of bias, the inspector general found lots of errors in the Carter Page surveillance applications. Basic errors. Shocking errors, given the layers of review and oversight. These were things that should have been caught, like misstatements of the FBI's relationship with a source, changes in the accounts offered by sources, or the existence of evidence that contradicted what we were telling the court. The review found seventeen significant errors. The inspector general didn't find evidence that they were intentional or motivated by bias, but many of them he simply couldn't explain.

He then set out to see if this was a problem with the Page case or something broader. It was much broader. In more than two dozen unrelated cases, the inspector general found errors in the applications in every case. It seems most of them wouldn't have made a difference in the court's decision, but that didn't matter. Mistakes were everywhere. How could that be?

I don't know what the inspector general's answer will be to that question, but I have an educated guess, at least in part: the nature of the process killed accountability, reducing the necessary fear. When everyone's ass is on the line—from a case agent to the director and from a junior attorney to the attorney general—nobody's is really on the line. And when the work will never see the light of day, the fear of personal ruin drops out entirely. When the process, unlike in a criminal investigation, doesn't belong to a prosecutor and agent who will together create the application and then stand behind it, literally, in a federal judge's office, then nobody is sufficiently afraid of being wrong. And when the surveillance will never be challenged in open court, with an agent on the witness stand defending his work and a prosecutor on her feet arguing for it, nobody is sufficiently nervous. I expect I will never work in the Department of Justice or the FBI again, but if I were still there I would push to have a single Justice lawyer and a single FBI case agent together appear before a FISA judge and assume personal responsibility. Bureaucracy creates false comfort by distributing responsibility. It should work like the process for a criminal wiretap does. Nothing focuses the mind like a good pucker.

———

The first FISA court order for surveillance of Carter Page was obtained on October 21, just days before the Clinton investigation nightmare came back into my life. After assuring the American people that the investigation was finished and repeatedly saying the same thing under oath before Congress, I met Anthony Weiner's laptop in the last week of October. That device, which had been seized in an unrelated FBI criminal investigation in New York, belonged to the disgraced former congressperson married to Hillary Clinton's longtime aide Huma Abedin. The New York office sent word that it held tens of thousands of Clinton's emails and might hold the emails we had never found from her first months as secretary of state. My investigators told me the find was hugely significant, could possibly change the result of the case, and couldn't be evaluated before the election.

I faced two awful choices, but one of them was far worse than the other: I could tell Congress that what I said all summer was not true, or I could conceal the fact of our discovery and that we had reopened the investigation—which would likely leak from New York anyway. Our practice was always to try to avoid any action that might impact an election, but here our choices were both such actions. Telling Congress shortly before an election was a terrible thing, but better, in my view—then and still—than the catastrophic choice of perpetuating a lie to the American people and their representatives. Our institution, built on a commitment to truth, could never be trusted again; we could always be hiding something. In a carefully constructed and sparse letter, I informed Congress that we had restarted our investigation for a limited purpose, and our world caught on fire, burning only slightly less intensely after the team finished their review three days before the election and I informed Congress we were done, again.

Patrice followed the election-year politics very closely and, for reasons I understand, wanted a woman to be elected president. She had worried about the criticism I would take in July for announcing the end of the case alone. She thought it was a close call, as I did, but agreed the better path was to step away from the attorney general. In late October, Patrice saw my agony about the choices I faced. With tears in her eyes, she told me it was just too close to the election for me to be doing anything. I told her I agreed, but whatever I did would be doing something. She was in pain, and knew I was in pain, so there was very little conversation about it in our house. We talked about the kids, our aging parents, the dog, everything except politics. For the first time in my adult life, I didn't vote in a presidential election. I was tired on election night, and wanted to block it all out, so I went to bed early. Sometime after 2:00 A.M., Patrice climbed into bed and gently nudged me. "Trump won," she said quietly, kissing me good night. I went back to sleep. I would need the rest.

CHAPTER 15

IN LIKE FLYNN

*But the partisan activities of some attorneys general in this
century, combined with the unfortunate legacy of Watergate, have
given rise to an understandable public concern that some decisions
at Justice may be the products of favor, or pressure, or politics.*
ATTORNEY GENERAL GRIFFIN B. BELL, 1978
REMARKS TO ALL DEPARTMENT OF JUSTICE ATTORNEYS

THE LITTLE TABLE FOR TWO—SET in the middle of the
White House residence's Green Room—rattled me. Presidents didn't
have dinner alone with FBI directors. At least not since Hoover and
Nixon hung out together. When President Trump called at the end
of his first week in office to invite me to dinner, I assumed it was a
group thing. I was wrong. This wasn't about team-building, in any
normal sense.

Early in the meal, he raised the prospect of "making a change"
at the FBI. I responded that I agreed he could fire the FBI director any time he wished, but that I wanted to stay and do a job I loved
and thought I was doing well in the fourth year of a ten-year term.
Because I sensed where this was going, I added that he could count
on me as being "reliable" in one way—I would always tell him the

truth. That wasn't what he was looking for. A short time later, he made clear what he wanted in exchange for my staying as director: "I need loyalty. I expect loyalty."

I responded with total silence and an unblinking stare for two or three seconds, an eternity at a table for two in the center of the Green Room. No president since Watergate, when the danger of the Department of Justice and the FBI becoming presidential fiefdoms was laid bare before the American people, had asked such a thing. Leaders of Justice and the FBI were disgraced by Watergate, and the president was forced to resign because he tried to obstruct justice. The country and its leaders had learned searing lessons from that nightmare.

The American people wanted separation, some distance between the chief executive and the chief investigator; that's why, after J. Edgar Hoover's death, their representatives in Congress created a symbolic ten-year term for the FBI director—to ensure nobody stayed for almost fifty years, as Hoover had, but also to extend the director past any president's tenure to create distance. Justice could not be done, it could not be credible, if the leaders of the institution were the president's consiglieri.

As a result, no president since Nixon would eat alone with the FBI director, lest someone wrongly conclude it was a bid for personal loyalty, an effort to close the distance. But here we were, as if gathered in the widow's tiny living room above the Ravenite Social Club. Here, the boss could talk—get a little loose—about what really mattered to him. Distance be damned. He wanted loyalty.

Looking back, my two or three seconds of silence doomed me. I tried to interrupt him during the series of monologues that followed to try to explain the importance of the distance, to recount how President Obama had stressed it when interviewing me for the job. I tried to appeal to his practical side, warning him of the paradoxical

mistake of trying to hold the Justice Department close to avoid problems, which undercuts its credibility and actually increases problems
for the president. It made no difference. He didn't care about any
of that. He wasn't interested in reservoirs or blindfolded statues. He
wanted one thing. Near the end of dinner, he demanded it again.

"I need loyalty."

I paused again. "You will always get honesty from me," I said.

He paused. "That's what I want, honest loyalty," he said.

I paused. "You will get that from me," I said, desperate to end our
standoff, thinking that maybe honest loyalty sounded enough like the
thing he wanted—but would never get from me.

I was kidding myself. There was no compromise possible, no mud-
dling through. I was a dead man walking. It was just a question of
when his distaste for my lack of personal allegiance would end things.
It wouldn't be long.

I wasn't supposed to be alone with him again on Valentine's Day. It
was a group meeting, a scheduled February 14, 2017, counterterrorism briefing of President Trump in the Oval Office. As usual, he held
forth from behind the desk, and a group of us sat in a semicircle of
about six chairs facing him on the other side. He ended the meeting by telling the group that he wanted to talk to me alone. When
the participants, including my boss—then–Attorney General Jeff
Sessions—were gone, Trump made clear why he had been distracted
during my terrorism briefing.

"I want to talk about Mike Flynn," he said. Flynn, his national
security adviser, had been forced to resign the previous day. I didn't
know Flynn well, but had testified alongside him in 2014 when he
served as director of the Defense Intelligence Agency. Flynn, who
was a retired U.S. Army general, had spoken to the Russian am-

bassador to the United States multiple times during late December 2016, to seek the Russians' help in derailing a United Nations resolution—which the Obama administration was not going to veto—condemning Israel for the expansion of its settlements in occupied territory, and also to urge the Russians not to escalate their response to Obama administration sanctions imposed as a result of Russian interference in the 2016 election. The conversations about sanctions had become the subject of intense public interest after they were reported in the media in early January and Vice President–Elect Mike Pence went on television to deny Flynn had talked about sanctions with the Russians. Pence said he knew this because he had talked to Flynn.

At the FBI in December 2016, we were going to close our investigation of Flynn, which began in late July of that election year as we were trying to figure out whether anyone associated with the Trump campaign had taken the Russians up on their offer of dirt on Hillary Clinton. We looked at Flynn as a possible suspect because he had traveled to Russia in 2015 for a paid speech for Russia's main international propaganda platform after being forced out as director of the Defense Intelligence Agency. He sat at the dinner with Vladimir Putin—strange behavior for a retired senior military intelligence officer. But in five months of looking, we hadn't found anything that went beyond suspicions and actually implicated Flynn. I was keen not to have an open counterintelligence investigation of a new president's national security adviser simply because we hadn't gotten around to closing the file. I told my staff that, if there was a basis to keep the Flynn case open, fine, but they should otherwise close it before he took office.

Then, before the file was closed, we discovered Flynn's extensive and unusual conversations with the Russian ambassador. The Russians had reacted strangely by not retaliating for sanctions imposed by President Obama after their interference in the 2016 election. All members of the intelligence community—which included the FBI—were asked to look for information that might explain the odd Russian passivity. In tapes of our routine surveillance of Russian diplomats in the United States, we found Flynn's calls with the Russian ambassador. And then Flynn apparently lied to the vice president and other senior leaders about those conversations, lies Pence repeated publicly. Something didn't smell right. Why would a retired general with Russia connections lie about talking to the Russians just after they interfered to defeat Hillary Clinton and elect Donald Trump? The best way to cut through the smell quickly was to talk to Flynn and ask him what was going on. I told the deputy director to see if Flynn was willing to sit down with agents and be interviewed.

I decided not to tell the acting attorney general, Sally Yates, in advance, something I knew would irritate her. I didn't need permission and, as I later explained to her, if the interview turned out to be significant, my taking responsibility would make it harder for Trump to claim it was some kind of last-gasp political move by departing Obama administration appointees like Yates. They could only blame me, and I was staying. And involving the lawyers at Main Justice would also risk bogging the whole thing down in bureaucratic protocol. I wanted to cut through the noise and find out what was going on, if Flynn was willing. He was, and met with the agents at the White House, repeating what he had told the vice president: he had never talked to the ambassador about Russian sanctions or the United Nations vote. The agents tried hard to keep him from lying to them. They pressed him, using words and phrases from the tapes of those conversations. He stuck to his denials.

I was mystified. Flynn's denials were so strange, when he surely knew it was all on tape, that I withheld judgment on whether he was intentionally lying. Maybe he had some kind of brain disease. Maybe he was drunk when he spoke to the Russian ambassador from his Dominican Republic beach vacation. To accuse someone of lying requires proof of both falsity and intention. There was no doubt Flynn's statements were false, but maybe there was something I couldn't see that undermined attributing intention to his falsehoods. I would learn later, from Special Counsel Robert Mueller's 2019 report, that Flynn lied because he thought the president wanted him to, but I could see none of that on Valentine's Day. We needed to continue to investigate, which we were doing when Trump cleared the room.

The day before, February 13, Trump had forced Flynn to resign because he had lied to Vice President Pence. He also knew Flynn had lied to the FBI. The president began by saying General Flynn hadn't done anything wrong in speaking with the Russians, but he had to let him go because he had misled the vice president. He added that he had other concerns about Flynn. I said nothing.

After a long detour into the problem of leaks of classified information, the president returned to the topic of Mike Flynn, saying, "He is a good guy and has been through a lot." He repeated that General Flynn hadn't done anything wrong on his calls with the Russians, but had misled the vice president.

He then said, "I hope you can see your way clear to letting this go, to letting Flynn go. He is a good guy. I hope you can let this go."

Trump knew Flynn was making false statements about his conversations with the Russian ambassador in December because the Department of Justice told the White House counsel. The president was directing me to drop any investigation of Flynn in connection with false statements about his conversations with the Russian ambassador in December. Nobody would get that break—especially when the lies were about a country that had just attacked our democracy. And no president who cared about the credibility of Justice would make that demand.

I only agreed that "he is a good guy," or seemed to be from what I knew of him. I did not say I would "let this go."

Trump showed no reaction to my reply and returned briefly to the problem of leaks. The conversation ended and I got up and left the Oval Office.

I was not going to drop a criminal investigation of a senior government official, even if the president told me to. That would undermine everything the Department of Justice represented. The core value of the department was that it cared only about the truth, not friendship, or party, or presidential favor. The reservoir of trust that the institution depended upon had been filled by following the facts, not cutting breaks for the privileged. I would never do it. He would have to fire me first.

For three months, I tried not to get fired. I tried to limit my contact with the president—avoiding the "Eye of Sauron," as I explained it to my staff, all of whom got my *Lord of the Rings* reference. I urged Attorney General Sessions and Rod Rosenstein, the new deputy attorney general, to serve as a buffer between me and Trump. I was determined to keep my head down and focus on the most important things I was doing with my ten-year term: trying to change leadership culture at the FBI and working to attract more women and people of color to the organization and into leadership. These were the ways I hoped to make a lasting difference for the organization. They were the reason I flew to Los Angeles on May 9, 2017, to host a diversity recruiting event for hundreds of talented young professionals, people I hoped would be future special agents.

Trump fired me that day, before I got to the recruiting event. I learned about it on television. Trump claimed he acted based on a memo from Deputy Attorney General Rosenstein summarizing criticism of my decisions during the investigation into Hillary Clinton's handling of classified information. The next day, chortling with Russian leaders in a private Oval Office meeting, Trump confirmed what I already knew—the memo about the Clinton case was a fraud and a cover for Trump's real reason for firing me: the investigation into Russian interference in the 2016 election and the possibility that Americans associated with his campaign worked with the Russians.

Eight days after I was fired, Rosenstein appointed Special Counsel Robert Mueller to investigate "any links and/or coordination between the Russian government and individuals associated with the campaign of President Donald Trump" and any efforts to obstruct justice in connection with that investigation.

Mueller worked silently for almost two years, until Friday, March 22, 2019, when he gave his 448-page report to Attorney General William P. Barr. On Sunday, March 24, Barr wrote to key members of the Senate and House of Representatives—in a letter that was immediately made public by Congress—informing them that the investigation "did not find that the Trump campaign or anyone associated with it conspired or coordinated with Russia in its efforts to influence the 2016 presidential election." Barr added that, with respect to the investigation into whether President Trump obstructed justice, Mueller "determined not to make a traditional prosecutorial judgment" and "did not draw a conclusion—one way or the other—as to whether the examined conduct constituted obstruction," thereby leaving it to Barr "to determine whether the conduct described in the report constitutes a crime." And he did that. The evidence, he wrote, "is not sufficient to establish that the President committed an obstruction-of-justice offense."

Barr pledged to move forward quickly to determine what parts of the Mueller report could be made public. In an extraordinary move for the reticent former FBI director, Mueller pushed back, writing to

Barr three days later that the March 24, 2019, letter "did not fully capture the context, nature, and substance of this Office's work and conclusions." As a result, Mueller wrote, "There is now public confusion about critical aspects of the results of the investigation," which, Mueller noted, "threatens to undermine a central purpose for which the Department appointed a Special Counsel: to assure full public confidence in the outcome of the investigations."

Barr was not done undermining that central purpose. He said he had been misunderstood. In another letter to Congress, he blamed the media, which had "mischaracterized" his letter as "a summary" of Mueller's work. He had intended no such thing. He was working hard to release the Mueller report.

Three weeks later, minutes before the public would have the opportunity to read Mueller's 448-page report, Barr decided the American people needed his views of it, so he held a press conference to offer his summary, which he also offered in another letter to Congress.

Thanks to Mueller's good work, he said, we now know that the Russians who interfered in our presidential election "did not have the cooperation of President Trump or the Trump campaign—or the knowing assistance of any other Americans for that matter." According to Barr, the "bottom line" was a sweeping rejection of speculation that Americans had worked with Russians: "After nearly two years of investigation, thousands of subpoenas, and hundreds of warrants and witness interviews, the Special Counsel confirmed that the Russian government sponsored efforts to illegally interfere with the 2016 presidential election but did not find that the Trump campaign or other Americans colluded in those schemes."

According to Barr, the results for obstruction of justice were similarly clear. Barr and Deputy Attorney General Rosenstein "concluded that the evidence developed by the Special Counsel is not sufficient to establish that the President committed an obstruction-of-justice offense." He reminded the American people that Trump had been right all along that "there was in fact no collusion." Trump, he explained, was understandably angered by the investigations and press speculation based on illegal leaks. Yet, despite that understandable frustration, the president—whose refusal to be interviewed by investigators Barr did not mention—had offered complete cooperation to Mueller, with "unfettered access" to evidence, and "took no act that in fact deprived the Special Counsel of the documents and witnesses necessary to complete his investigation."

In light of the attorney general's statements, the report itself would come as a shock to fair-minded people who actually read it. In the report, Mueller didn't say he found no evidence the Russians worked with the Trump campaign. He found lots of "links"—none of which were reported to the FBI so it might stop Russia's interference. Among those was a June 2016 Trump Tower meeting between Russians and Trump campaign leaders that had been billed to the Trump team as an offer of "documents and information that would incriminate Hillary and her dealings with Russia" as "part of Russia and its government's support for Mr. Trump." He also found a tight connection between Trump's former campaign leader, Paul Manafort, and a Russian intelligence officer, to whom Manafort funneled inside information about the campaign.

But Mueller said he didn't find sufficient evidence to prove a crime:

In sum, the investigation established multiple links between Trump Campaign officials and individuals tied to the Russian government. Those links included Russian offers of assistance to the Campaign. In some instances, the Campaign was receptive to the offer, while in other instances the Campaign officials shied away. Ultimately, the investigation did not

establish that the Campaign coordinated or conspired with
the Russian government in its election-interference activities.

In short, Mueller found plenty of noxious, choking smoke, but couldn't
prove a legal fire.

In turning to whether Trump obstructed justice, Mueller accepted
the department's decades-old legal conclusion that he couldn't indict
a sitting president. As a result, he "determined not to make a traditional prosecutorial judgment . . . recogniz[ing] that a federal criminal accusation against a sitting President would place burdens on the
President's capacity to govern and potentially preempt constitutional
processes for addressing presidential misconduct."

Therefore, Mueller "determined not to apply an approach that
could potentially result in a judgment that the President committed
crimes" because "[f]airness concerns counseled against potentially
reaching that judgment when no charges can be brought." But,
because Trump could be prosecuted after he leaves office, Mueller said,
he "conducted a thorough factual investigation in order to preserve
the evidence when memories were fresh and documentary materials
were available."

Because Mueller was experienced enough to see that unprincipled
people might distort his reticence as exoneration, he said it was no
such thing: "[I]f we had confidence after a thorough investigation
of the facts that the President clearly did not commit obstruction of
justice, we would so state. Based on the facts and the applicable legal
standards, however, we are unable to reach that judgment. Accord-
ingly, while this report does not conclude that the President committed a crime, it also does not exonerate him."

Yes it did, said Barr and Trump, endlessly. No collusion. No obstruction. Complete and total exoneration. Anyone who read Mueller's
report knew these were lies, told, predictably, by Donald Trump. It

was less predictable that those same lies would also be told by the attorney general of the United States.

In some sense, though, Trump and Barr are hard to blame because they are a certain kind of person, acting in character. Instead, at least some of the blame lies in an unexpected direction, on a person who couldn't be more different from Trump and Barr. The truth is that Bob Mueller's choices made it possible for Trump and Barr to mislead the American people.

Mueller tried to do something principled and fair, which is his nature. If he was bound by the principle that the Department of Justice couldn't indict a sitting president—and he concluded he was—it would be unfair to write a report accusing Trump of a crime for which Trump could not seek vindication through a trial. Better to assemble the evidence for a future prosecutor and for the current Congress. But in assembling that evidence, Mueller accomplished the very harm he was seeking to avoid, and at tremendous cost in public confusion and loss of public confidence in the Department of Justice.

The evidence Mueller laid out in excruciating detail accused the president, for all practical purposes, of criminal obstruction of justice. Yes, Barr and Rosenstein claimed to have concluded—with lightning speed and without interviewing Trump—that he lacked the required bad intention, but the report is damning in its breadth and detail, as hundreds of former federal prosecutors saw instantly and said publicly.

Yet somehow, Mueller managed to be unfair to both Trump and the Department of Justice. He wrote a report that smeared the president with devastating detail, but, by not formally accusing the president, while also not exonerating the president, he confused people and left his work susceptible to cynical distortion. And the form of his report only made it worse.

As Winston Churchill once said, "This report, by its very length, defends itself against the risk of being read." Few people read the 448 pages of single-spaced twelve-point Times New Roman type with 2,375 footnotes. Almost nobody read the only slightly less dense executive summary. Americans no longer get their information that way, if they ever did. They get their information in smaller packages—from sound bites, pithy excerpts, tweets.

Mueller did the right thing by presenting a detailed report, as the Department of Justice has long done, but he chose to submit his unreadable—and unread—report and then go away without a sound (with the exception of reticent testimony—"I refer you to the report"—months later that added nothing to public understanding). In contrast, Bill Barr went to his keyboard to write pithy letters to Congress, and then to the microphone to tell the American people what was what. Citizens of goodwill can be forgiven for not knowing that Barr was defrauding the American people and aiding and abetting Trump's outright lies about the report. In a way, that's the fault of Robert Mueller and his team.

If, as Mueller wrote in his mild pushback to Barr's first fraudulent letter, he was appointed "to assure full public confidence in the outcome of the investigation," then he owed it to the American people to complete his work in a way that fostered full confidence. And people can't have confidence in things they don't know. I learned from personal experience that critics have an impressive ability to see the past clearly, so I hesitate to offer hindsight judgments about what Mueller should have done; except that he could have found a way to speak to the American people in their language, which is not the language of footnotes and twelve-point Times New Roman. Department policy and tradition gave him plenty of flexibility to speak in the public interest. He chose not to, and, in the end, the only voices most Americans heard were lying to them. No truth, no transparency, and Justice paid the price in lost trust.

Last year, a federal judge in Washington, D.C., declined to accept assurances by Department of Justice attorneys that portions of
the Mueller report that remained blacked out were properly withheld
from the public. In essence, the judge told the department lawyers
that, given the way Barr had acted, he could no longer trust them:

> [T]he Court cannot reconcile certain public representations
> made by Attorney General Barr with the findings in the
> Mueller Report. The inconsistencies between Attorney General
> Barr's statements, made at a time when the public did not have
> access to the redacted version of the Mueller Report to assess the
> veracity of his statements, and portions of the redacted version
> of the Mueller Report that conflict with those statements cause
> the Court to seriously question whether Attorney General Barr
> made a calculated attempt to influence public discourse about
> the Mueller Report in favor of President Trump despite certain
> findings in the redacted version of the Mueller Report to the
> contrary.

Attorney General Barr's actions changed how the judge thought about
the Department of Justice: "These circumstances generally, and Attorney General Barr's lack of candor specifically, call into question Attorney General Barr's credibility and in turn, the Department's. . . ."

Water was pouring from the reservoir. It kept draining.

In November 2017, six months after I was fired, Michael Flynn agreed
to plead guilty to lying to the FBI and promised to cooperate with
Mueller's prosecutors, in exchange for dropped charges of other crimes
and the possibility of a reduced sentence. Over the following two
years, he admitted before two different federal judges that he was

guilty of lying, knew at the time he was lying, and agreed that the government could convict him of it. It turns out he wasn't drunk and didn't have a stroke. He lied, brazenly, because he thought the boss wanted him to.

The Mueller report explains that Trump was angered by the first news story that Flynn had spoken to the Russians about the sanctions imposed by Obama, asking, "What the hell is this all about?" His reaction was curious because there was good reason to think he knew what it was about, but the White House chief of staff dutifully told Flynn that Trump was angry, advising him to "kill the story," which Flynn did by telling another White House aide to deny it to the reporter. The story was going to be that Flynn never discussed sanctions with the Russians, and he stuck to it, even when the FBI asked.

Then, on May 7, 2020, in the middle of a pandemic, Barr's Department of Justice moved to dismiss the case against the already-convicted Flynn, arguing that his false statements were not "material" to anything the FBI had a legitimate basis to investigate. The only signatory was a political appointee, the then–acting United States Attorney for the District of Columbia, who weeks earlier had been one of Attorney General Barr's personal staff members. The career prosecutors who had handled the case for two years refused to sign the document, and one of them formally withdrew from the case.

The arguments made by Bill Barr's handpicked representative were, in the words of a former federal judge appointed by the trial court to respond, "so irregular, and so obviously pretextual," as to "constitute clear evidence of gross prosecutorial abuse. They reveal an unconvincing effort to disguise as legitimate a decision to dismiss that is based solely on the fact that Flynn is a political ally of President Trump."

The retired judge summarized the absurdity of the government's new claim:

At the time of Flynn's interview with the FBI, it was conducting a counterintelligence investigation into possible coordination between individuals associated with the Trump campaign and the Russian government. Flynn was a Trump advisor with ties to the Kremlin's "principal international propaganda outlet," who had made unusual backchannel requests to Russia's most senior government official in the U.S., then concealed those communications from high-level U.S. officials. When the FBI repeatedly asked Flynn about those communications, he chose to lie about them—just as he had lied to various senior White House officials. That is about as straightforward a case of materiality as a prosecutor, court, or jury will ever see.

Much about the government's new position was incomprehensible, but not its origin. Since telling me to "let it go" in February 2017, President Trump had been trying to find allies at the Department of Justice who would do what he wanted in cases involving his friends. For Flynn, Trump mounted a media campaign that included more than one hundred tweets or retweets, making clear that he was closely following Flynn's case, hated those who had investigated and prosecuted Flynn—"dirty, filthy cops at the top of the FBI"—and wanted Justice to let it go. It was all a scam, the president said endlessly, engineered to ensnare Flynn, who probably hadn't lied anyway—despite Trump having fired him for lying.

The tweetstorm for Flynn presciently predicted the narrative of the Department of Justice's unprecedented motion to dismiss Flynn's case. It was as if Trump wrote it, and so poorly that it was, in the words of the retired judge, "riddled with inexplicable and elementary errors of law and fact." Sloppy or not, it was Trump's second successful effort to change how the department approached a criminal case of personal interest to him.

Earlier in 2020, when Trump took to Twitter to urge the department to reduce its sentencing recommendation for his long-time associate Roger Stone—convicted of lying to the special counsel and Congress during investigation of the 2016 Russian interference effort—Attorney General Barr publicly lamented that Trump's "public statements and tweets" about pending cases "make it impossible to do my job and to assure the courts and the prosecutors in the department that we're doing our work with integrity." To careful observers, though, Barr was lamenting that Trump, by showing the world what he was up to, was making it hard for Barr to do Trump's bidding. Justice is supposed to be evenhanded, nonpartisan. Friends of the president aren't supposed to get special treatment.

Trump went public with his demands for a reduced sentence for his friend Stone just after Barr removed Jessie Liu, the well-regarded United States Attorney in D.C., and installed as the acting U.S. Attorney his staffer, who promptly reversed career prosecutors and slashed, without justification, the recommended sentence for Stone. It was another move nobody had ever seen before, and done to benefit a crony of the president. To their great credit, the career prosecutors on the case also refused to participate and withdrew; one of the four quit government. But Barr and his staffer did it anyway, because the president wanted it done.

The insult to justice didn't end there, because Donald Trump couldn't take the chance of Roger Stone's going to jail; he knew too much. Stone had gotten a lighter sentence than career prosecutors sought, but he was still sentenced to three years. As the sentencing judge explained, Stone was "prosecuted for covering up for the President." His crimes were serious, she explained, because "truth still exists. The truth still matters. Roger Stone's insistence that it doesn't, his belligerence, his pride in his own lies are a threat to our most fundamental institutions, to the very foundation of our democracy."

Stone may have been belligerent, but he expected something in exchange for obstructing justice for Trump, just not from the judge. Days before he was to report to prison for lying to protect Trump, Stone told an interviewer: "I had twenty-nine or thirty conversations with Trump during the campaign period. He knows I was under enormous pressure to turn on him. It would have eased my situation considerably. But I didn't. They wanted me to play Judas. I refused." Stone stood up for Trump. He lied for him and expected to be taken care of.

An hour later, Trump rewarded Stone's commitment to their personal *cosa nostra* by commuting Stone's sentence so he would never see the inside of a jail cell. It was a shocking-enough attack on the justice system that Bill Barr, his loyal attorney general, let it be known he had recommended against it and thought Stone's sentence "righteous." Robert Mueller broke his silence to pen a newspaper opinion piece. He wrote that the investigation, despite Barr's dark insinuations and Trump's relentless attacks, was both legitimate and important. Stone lied about his contacts with Russian intelligence officers, behavior that Mueller said "strikes at the core of the government's efforts to find the truth and hold wrongdoers accountable." But, no matter, Roger Stone was a free man.

With the Stone and Flynn cases, Trump and Barr had changed the architecture of justice. The traditional blindfold on Lady Justice was gone. It had been replaced with a MAGA hat.

CHAPTER 16

THE WEB

Falsehood flies and truth comes limping after it, so that when
[people] come to be undeceived, it is too late.
JONATHAN SWIFT

IT WAS NEVER GOING TO WORK BETWEEN ME
and Donald Trump. We were too different. When I was learning painful lessons about the need to disclose the full truth—even about small
things like the denominations of a drug dealer's cash or a second marriage in the Witness Protection Program or a mobster's FBI watch—
when I was learning to never make an argument for the government
I didn't fully believe in, he was taking a different approach in his
career, which his ghostwriter described in *The Art of the Deal:*

> [A] little hyperbole never hurts. People want to believe that
> something is the biggest and the greatest and the most
> spectacular. I call it truthful hyperbole. It's an innocent form
> of exaggeration, and a very effective form of promotion.

I had grown up in an institution for which a little hyperbole always
hurts, because it is a lie. Maybe a certain kind of real estate developer

feels comfortable saying his building is taller than it really is, but in the Department of Justice that's a firing offense, not an effective form of promotion.

I had grown up in an institution that depended upon the trust of the American people. The goal of everything we did was to foster that trust. We gave the country details about our work so they would see us as something separate and honest, so they would believe us at doorways and in courtrooms. We explained why we were in the Black community pursuing gun crimes to save lives and we listened to concerns and questions. We forced our witnesses to admit things nobody would have known otherwise. We knew lying was a threat to the heart of the justice system.

I had grown up in an institution that was also human, so regularly made mistakes. To protect our reservoir of trust and credibility, we admitted those errors, whether they were about a case precedent we had misremembered or about a racist psychopath who got a gun because we failed on a background check or about innocent people who were in jail because we exaggerated our science. These things hurt, but what Americans thought of us was everything, so we told the whole truth. We also worked not to repeat our mistakes, because our institution was rooted in trying to do things the right way.

Donald Trump could not understand such an institution. His life, his career, was about how things look, not how they are. What mattered was whether the deal closed and he got his money. Say what needs to be said, because winning was the thing. Maybe that bank or that contractor or that employee would resolve never to work with him again, but there were always other banks, contractors, and workers. Winning now is what matters.

I was raised in an institution where winning is not the thing, a place governed by values that even the Supreme Court, in describing the role of a federal prosecutor in 1935 (*Berger v. United States*), conceded are a little odd:

> [H]e is in a peculiar and very definite sense the servant of the law, the twofold aim of which is that guilt shall not escape or innocence suffer. He may prosecute with earnestness and vigor—indeed he should do so. But while he may strike hard blows, he is not at liberty to strike foul ones. It is as much his duty to refrain from improper methods calculated to produce a wrongful conviction as it is to use every legitimate means to bring about a just one.

I was raised in an institution that aspires to use its power without regard to privilege or race or connections, a place where the work can't ever be about friendship or loyalty, or we will never be trusted again. A place where I fought to maintain the perception and the reality that my New York prosecutors were not part of the Washington political scrum, where we appointed special prosecutors when the American people might reasonably question our independence, where presidents knew not to drop the *s* and take interest in a case that would help them or their friends.

Everything about the institution of justice was threatened at that tiny table set in the middle of the Green Room. The president of the United States was not interested in fancy talk about people who were "in a peculiar and very definite sense the servant of the law." He wanted loyalty, he expected loyalty, not speeches about ancient oaths promising justice "without fear or favor, affection or ill-will." That's loser talk.

Trump spent two years trying to get the Justice Department he wanted. He told me to let Flynn go. I wouldn't. He twice asked me to announce publicly that he wasn't under investigation, something that was literally true at the time, but both misleading and likely to be short-lived, so I refused. He fired me, triggering the appointment of a special prosecutor whose work he relentlessly tried to obstruct, taking a flamethrower to the FBI and lamenting that his first attorney general, Jeff Sessions, was weak and wouldn't do his bidding.

In late 2018, he fired Sessions, and finally found his man in William P. Barr, who had already served as attorney general and deputy attorney general under President George H. W. Bush and went on to work as the general counsel of a major public company. Like other Department of Justice alumni, I said publicly at the time that, given Barr's prior service in the department in the 1980s and '90s, he was entitled to the benefit of the doubt. But I underweighted two things:

First, I didn't focus on the fact that Barr had never investigated or prosecuted a case; in serving only in senior roles at Main Justice, he never had the chance to make and learn from the mistakes of a young prosecutor, the ones that seared into you an understanding of the department's role in American life, the knowledge that you represent an idea, not an ordinary client.

And second, I missed the significance of the fact that, before he was chosen, private-citizen Barr had, in a way, auditioned for the job by penning an unsolicited memo to the Department of Justice criticizing the special counsel's pursuit of the president for obstruction of justice.

Maybe it was still fair to give the benefit of the doubt, but it quickly evaporated. Because here was a man who would show loyalty, who would let things go when Trump wanted them gone, who defamed his own department because Trump wanted it slimed.

I don't know why Attorney General Barr acted as he did. I may never know. How could an accomplished lawyer start channeling the president in using words like "no collusion" and FBI "spying"? Or darkly suggest—in improper press comments—that the government acted illegitimately in investigating Russian electoral interference, despite the fact that his own inspector general and the Republican-controlled Senate Select Committee on Intelligence said that wasn't true and, in the Senate's words, that Trump's campaign chair was a "grave counter-intelligence threat"? Or downplay acts of obstruction of justice as products of the president's being "frustrated and angry," something he would never say to justify the thousands of crimes prosecuted every day that are the product of frustration and anger?

How could he write and say things about the report by Robert Mueller that were so misleading they prompted written protest from the special counsel himself? How could he personally intervene to direct more lenient treatment for the president's friend Roger Stone and then order the abandonment of a case against Michael Flynn on transparently frivolous grounds, after Flynn twice pleaded guilty, treating those two Trump-world heroes in a way no criminal defendants had ever been treated?

I don't know for sure. People are complicated, so the answer is most likely complicated, as well. But I have some idea from months of seeing Trump up close and many more months of watching him shape others. Amoral leaders have a way of revealing the character of those around them. Sometimes what they reveal is inspiring. For example, James Mattis, the former secretary of defense, resigned over principle when Trump abandoned our beleaguered Kurdish allies in Syria, a concept so alien to Trump that it took days for the president to realize what had happened, before he could start lying about the man.

But more often, proximity to an amoral leader reveals something depressing. I think that's at least part of what happened with Barr. Accomplished people lacking inner strength couldn't resist the compromises necessary to survive Trump, and that added up to something they will never recover from and that damaged the institution they led. It takes character like Mattis's to avoid the damage.

It started with sitting silent while Trump lied, both in public and private, making those close to him complicit by their silence. In meetings with him, his assertions about what "everyone thinks" and what is "obviously true" washed over his audience, unchallenged, as they did at our Green Room dinner, because he was the president and he rarely stopped talking. As a result, Trump pulled all of those present into a silent circle of assent.

Speaking rapid-fire, leaving no opening for others to jump into the conversation, Trump made everyone a co-conspirator to his lies, or delusions. I felt it—the president building with his words a web of alternative reality and busily wrapping it around all of us in the room. I must have agreed that he had the largest inauguration crowd in history, because I didn't challenge that. Everyone must agree that he has been treated very unfairly. The web building never stopped.

From the private circle of assent, it moved to public displays of personal fealty at places like cabinet meetings. While the entire world watched, his subordinates did what everyone else around the table did—talked about how amazing the leader was and what an honor it was to be associated with him. Sure, they must have noticed that Mattis never actually praised the president, speaking instead of the honor of representing the men and women of our military. But he's a special case, right? Former marine general and all. No way the rest of them could get away with that. So they praised, while the world watched, and the web got tighter.

Next came Trump attacking institutions and values they held dear—things they always said must be protected and which they criticized past leaders for not supporting strongly enough. Yet they were silent. Because, after all, what were they supposed to say? He was the president of the United States.

They felt this happening. It bothered them, at least to some extent. But his outrageous conduct convinced them that they simply had to stay, to preserve and protect the people and institutions and values they held dear. Along with Republican members of Congress, they told themselves they were too important for this nation to lose, especially now.

They couldn't say this out loud—maybe not even to family—but in a time of emergency, with the nation led by a deeply unethical person, that would be their contribution, a personal sacrifice for America. They were smarter than Donald Trump, willing to play a long game for the country, and could pull it off where lesser leaders failed and got fired by tweet.

Of course, to stay, they had to be seen as being on his team, so they made further compromises. They used his language, praised his leadership, touted his commitment to values, gave special treatment to his friends. And then they were lost and the institutions they represented stained.

Then one of them was the attorney general of the United States, marching across a public square thick with noxious chemicals, violently cleared of protesters exercising their First Amendment rights on his order—all so the president could hold a Bible for the cameras. Maybe he was already lost, but the institution of Justice—devoted to truth, and transparency, and dependent upon the trust of the American people—grew still more soiled.

I confess part of me was relieved to be fired, to be away from Donald Trump and his web of lies, his endless demands for personal and institutional compromise. I felt relieved not to have the responsibility to lead the FBI in the face of smears and stains coming from Trump and later from his second attorney general. Of course, that small sense of relief at being fired was accompanied by stabs of guilt at leaving the people and institution I cared about behind and unprotected, at never completing the task of changing what the FBI looked like and how it was led. I had planned to stay, despite the fact that I dreaded working under Trump, because I owed that to the people of the FBI, to try to stand between them and a deeply unethical president. And there were no leaders at the Department of Justice with the strength and character to protect the FBI. Attorney General Sessions was hounded into irrelevance by Trump, and his deputy, Rod Rosenstein, who had acceded to Trump's demand for a memo to cover the truth about my firing, was afraid of mean tweets. So I felt stabbing guilt at leaving the place exposed, and sadness in the knowledge that I would likely never go back.

The emotion was compounded by the many FBI employees who sent me cards, letters, or gifts after I was fired. One employee who had begun offering "Comey Is My Homey" coffee mugs for sale (at cost) to her colleagues was told she could no longer use FBI email to take orders; the thousands of orders within the FBI had far exceeded the "minimal use" allowed under regulations. Maybe the most touching gift didn't involve me. Our beloved rescue dog, Benji, an ancient mutt of terrier ancestry, was a wanderer, which was how he had ended up in the Virginia adoption kennel where we found him. During my time as FBI director, he wandered out of gates, over walls, and down streets, with every outing and re-rescue by motorists and joggers captured by surveillance cameras. The FBI employees who spent four years watching Benji wander sent my family a picture book of his greatest escapes. When Benji died in 2018, it became a priceless family heirloom. People like that are why I was sad to be fired.

I was sad, but consoled myself with the knowledge that I wouldn't have lasted long anyway, not with a president for whom lying was as natural as breathing, and especially not once Trump found an attorney general who would attack the credibility of his own organization, who would do the president's bidding no matter the cost to the Justice Department. I would have defended our institution when the president and the attorney general lied about the FBI, when they defamed its people. I would have been fired sooner or later.

Many Americans of goodwill believe the Department of Justice and the FBI were part of a corrupt "deep state" plot to hurt Donald Trump's candidacy and presidency. Many of them believe I was a dirty cop, a dishonest leader who commanded that treasonous effort. They believe this because they have been told it, by the president of the United States, hundreds of times, echoed thousands of times by his boosters, including his final attorney general. They believe it even though it makes no sense given the events of 2016, when Democrats, with greater cause—although still wrongly—thought we were out to hurt Hillary Clinton while conducting our Trump-related investigations in complete secrecy. They believe it even in the face of repeated investigations that found no such thing. They believe it because Trump and Bill Barr always promised "the next investigation" would find the proof. Then, at long last, I and the other bad people would go to jail, as Trump demanded endlessly. Ordinary Americans have heard it so often that my Fox News–watching elderly mother-in-law regularly worried from her Iowa assisted-living apartment that I would be arrested. No matter how many times I told her with a laugh that it was all made up, all lies, she still worried. I understand why. Vladimir Lenin never visited Iowa, but he knew: "A lie repeated often enough becomes the truth."

It wasn't just Bill Barr's lies about the Mueller report or interventions to help Trump's friends that drained the reservoir. The four years of lying about the people of the FBI and the Department of Justice also lowered the water level. Each time a Fox News personality or member of Congress distorted the texts between two FBI employees who were having an affair to suggest that the FBI had acted with partisan motive—despite exhaustive investigation by the independent inspector general that found no such thing—water left the reservoir. Each time the president lied and said I had disclosed classified information to the media, water seeped out. Each time the attorney general said he didn't believe the inspector general's conclusion that the FBI's Russia investigation was properly opened, the reservoir shrank.

In the 1980s, a former cabinet secretary who was charged with crimes and then found not guilty asked, "Which office do I go to, to get my reputation back?" There is no such office. In the face of appalling compromise of the Department of Justice's nonpartisan values and the relentless lies about its work and people, there is no easy fix. The road back is long and steep.

EPILOGUE

Restoration

Time's glory is to calm contending kings, to unmask falsehood, and bring truth to light.
WILLIAM SHAKESPEARE

YES, THE WAY BACK TO TRUST WILL BE STEEP, but we know the way because the Department of Justice has traveled it before. Being honest and open with the American people will get you there. Truth and transparency lead to trust. It can be done. Edward Levi showed the way forty-five years ago.

Four people served as attorney general during the six years Richard Nixon was president. Two of them—including Nixon's closest friend and campaign manager, who served as his first attorney general—were later indicted and convicted of crimes committed for Nixon. He nominated a political loyalist to be FBI director after J. Edgar Hoover died, and installed him as acting director pending Senate confirmation (which, thankfully, never came). Eleven days after the Watergate break-in, the White House counsel brought that acting FBI director a package of documents, explaining they came from the

White House safe of E. Howard Hunt—designer of the break-in and chief of the Nixon dirty-tricks squad—and asked him to get rid of them. Nixon's chosen FBI leader did, by burning them in the fireplace of his Connecticut home. He also shared the FBI's files on the Watergate investigation with the White House, later acknowledging that he had not realized he was "dealing with individuals who were trying to sweep me into the very conspiracy that I was charged with investigating," a situation he called "a madman's horror."

The president tried to use the FBI and the CIA to shut down the Watergate investigation.

When that failed, he moved to fire the special prosecutor investigating him, leading to the "Saturday night massacre," the heroic departure of the attorney general and deputy attorney general who refused to carry out his order.

The stain wasn't limited to Watergate. At the same time, the American people learned of the FBI's decades-long abuse of its investigative and surveillance powers, its harassment of civil rights leaders, antiwar protesters, and student groups. The country discovered that the bureau had even tried to blackmail Martin Luther King into killing himself.

In the wake of Richard Nixon's resignation as president, the Justice Department was deeply soiled. Deservedly, it had lost the trust of the American people.

When Gerald Ford became president upon Nixon's resignation in disgrace, he knew restoration of the rule of law and the fair administration of justice were his highest priorities. He reached outside the government and asked Edward Levi, the sixty-three-year-old, bow tie–wearing president of the University of Chicago and longtime law professor, to serve as attorney general and save the department. It was an unusual choice. Levi's politics were unclear. As *The New York Times* wrote, "Some news accounts questioned whether he was best described as a conservative, liberal or libertarian. When he left office two years later, the answer was no clearer, but the question seemed mostly irrelevant." It was irrelevant to President Ford from the start. He needed a person of principle and stature to restore the department after years of partisan corruption.

Levi knew how hard it would be. He acknowledged he was taking office "in a time of change and corrosive skepticism and cynicism concerning the administration of justice." Public confidence in the department was everything to Levi. Nothing, he said, was worse than failing "to make clear by words and deed that our law is not an instrument of partisan purpose, and it is not to be used in ways which are careless of the higher values which are within all of us."

Levi delivered both the words and the deeds. He toured the country, constantly speaking about the department, admitting its faults, and explaining the values he intended to emphasize and protect. He gathered all the chief federal prosecutors to tell them: "The reinforcement of public confidence in the administration of justice cannot be a show thing, particularly when that confidence has been wounded. What has to count is both effectiveness and fairness in performance. What has to count also is our willingness to confront issues as they are . . . [and] take a new look at what we are doing."

He took that new look and was shocked by what he saw, especially in the FBI's caseload aimed at allegedly subversive American citizens and their organizations—under an umbrella called COIN-TELPRO. "Those [investigations] that were not foolish were outrageous," he said, and he pushed for disclosure of FBI activities and the first-ever guidelines regulating the scope of the FBI's tactics, such as surveillance and investigation of domestic political groups. The "Levi guidelines," which resulted in the closure of most FBI political investigations, were not required by statute or the courts; in the late 1970s, the infiltration of domestic organizations was not seen as impinging

on legal rights. But Levi believed self-restraint was essential to public confidence, so he imposed it on the FBI that Hoover built. He
also supported changing the law, endorsing legislation to regulate
the government's use of electronic surveillance in national security
cases—leading to the birth of FISA.

It wasn't enough to change the rules and implement new training.
He had to change culture, the powerful, invisible force that guides
all human organizations. Every organization is guided by its culture,
which experts divide into three layers: artifacts, espoused beliefs,
and underlying assumptions. Artifacts are the symbols and signs of
an organization—its flags, founding documents, slogans, and ceremonies. You can see those from a distance. Espoused beliefs are the
things the organization says it stands for—the mission statements,
lists of values, rules—and are also visible from the outside. Underlying assumptions represent the bedrock of culture, the way things
are really done, no matter what they tell you in training, the things
you can't discover from recruiting posters and orientation lectures, the
things you learn only after you've been there awhile. Healthy organizations know the power of that bottom level, and work to be sure
it lines up with the symbols, rules, and speeches up above, to ensure
that "the way things are really done around here" is the way ethical
leaders want them done.

Levi had to change the rules, post them around the Department
of Justice, and follow that with lofty speeches appealing to core values. But that would not be enough to reach the bottom layer, the level
of the unspoken, the unacknowledged. Trying to make the Department of Justice nonpartisan by instructing its employees to be nonpartisan would be like trying to raise good children by having them
read the penal code. They need more. They need to see that you mean
it, that you act it; then they will believe the training. Levi needed to
walk a certain way, hire a certain way, dress a certain way, live a certain

way. In every moment, public and private, he needed to show them so they would believe and imitate. He knew all this. "A great leader radiates the values of the institution," he said.

In just two years, he saved the place. When he left office after Jimmy Carter succeeded Ford as president, Levi could offer words of well-earned satisfaction: "I leave confident that the morale and purpose of this Department are high. We have shown that the administration of justice can be fair, can be effective, can be non-partisan."

But despite the confidence, Levi knew the work was never done, because he knew organizational culture. The challenge of culture is that it is so hard to see, taste, and feel. Culture goes bad the way a room's air goes bad; if you step into an unhealthy culture from the outside, it stinks to high heaven, but in many cases, those inside don't even notice. A healthy culture needs constant attention, which is why Levi left with a warning about the values of transparency and truth and independence: "These are goals which can never be won for all time. They must always be won anew. I know you will be steadfast in your adherence to them."

These last few years, the leaders of the Department of Justice have not been steadfast.

Saving Justice will be simple, in a way. The new president just needs to find leaders who will radiate the values of the institution.

The task for the next attorney general will be easier than Edward Levi's after Watergate, when he faced an institution with deeply problematic unspoken assumptions about the use of its power. After decades of abuse and six years of Nixonian corruption, the place was broken.

The good news is that the department Levi and his successors built over nearly fifty years remains fundamentally healthy and apolitical. Donald Trump and his followers didn't have enough time to destroy the calm waters of the sound; sure, they urged the partisan ocean water in, but they didn't have time to swamp the apolitical sound. The unspoken assumptions about the right way to behave—carried in the hearts of tens of thousands of career Justice employees—remain the foundation of the department.

There is no "deep state" as Trump used that term, but there is a deep culture at Justice, put down into bedrock since Watergate. We saw a sample of it in the career prosecutors who refused to participate in the corrupt gifts to Trump cronies Roger Stone and Michael Flynn. Those lawyers represent career Justice employees, who share a set of deeply rooted assumptions—that they should seek and speak the truth, without fear or favor, and without regard to politics or privilege. Department of Justice and FBI employees are hungry to return to the quiet work of nonpartisan law enforcement. Thousands of them have stayed the course while in agony about the leadership above them. The next attorney general needs only to encourage those quiet heroes to be what they have long been.

The bigger challenge will be restoring the trust of the American people, after those on the right have internalized so many lies about the institution and those on the left have seen it hijacked at the highest level by the Trump crowd. The next attorney general must be someone the American people—no matter how they voted—see as above the partisan and committed to apolitical justice. And the next attorney general will need to accomplish that in the face of a storm of lies from Fox News personalities and Donald Trump's next self-aggrandizing venture. To do it, the attorney general needs to lift the Department of Justice above the partisan scrum.

This is not the time to expand the case against Michael Flynn—despite the outrages committed by the president and his attorney general to help their ally. It also isn't the time for the Justice Department to pursue a criminal investigation of Donald Trump, no matter how compelling the road map left behind by Special Counsel Mueller, or how powerful the evidence strewn across his history of porn stars and financial fraud. Although those cases might be righteous in a vacuum, the mission of the next attorney general must be fostering the trust of the American people that the institution is not a tool of political payback.

Gerald Ford pardoned Richard Nixon to end America's national 1970s nightmare of division, recrimination, and institutional abuse. Ford likely lost his election bid as a result, because there was a widespread hunger to hold a criminal president to account, but history has judged Ford to have been wiser than his time. Our next attorney general must be similarly farsighted, seeing the national interest in a Department of Justice apart from political tribe.

But I might be wrong. There are powerful arguments that the rule of law requires that a criminal chief executive be held to account and that Watergate was different in a critical way: Nixon resigned the presidency after his crimes were exposed, and he also accepted President Gerald Ford's pardon, an act the Supreme Court long ago said amounts to a confession of guilt. In fact, for the rest of his life Ford carried in his wallet a portion of the text of that 1915 Supreme Court decision. By pardoning a resigned president, Ford had held him accountable in a way that Trump would not be, even were he to be pardoned after losing reelection. That might not be enough accountability in Trump's case. Or it may be, especially if local prosecutors in New York charge Trump for a legacy of financial fraud.

Whatever the new president and his attorney general decide, they should show their work to the country. To foster trust, they must be transparent and explain to the American people why they are not prosecuting Trump or others in his world. If they make a different decision, to pursue some or all of the unaddressed crimes, they should explain that as well, to demonstrate they aren't engaged in political payback.

In 1974, President Ford took the extraordinary step of testifying before Congress, appearing before the House Judiciary Committee a month after pardoning Nixon. It was, Ford said, an act "that has no firm precedent in the whole history of presidential relations with the Congress. Yet, I am here not to make history, but to report on history." The president sat alone at the witness table and explained himself to Congress and the American people, saying he pardoned the departed Nixon because "I wanted to do all I could to shift our attentions from the pursuit of a fallen president to the pursuit of the urgent needs of a rising nation."

In that October 1974 testimony, President Ford spoke to his moment, but also to ours:

> We would needlessly be diverted from meeting those
> challenges if we as a people were to remain sharply divided over
> whether to indict, bring to trial, and punish a former president,
> who already is condemned to suffer long and deeply in the
> shame and disgrace brought upon the office he held. Surely,
> we are not a revengeful people. We have often demonstrated a
> readiness to feel compassion and to act out of mercy. As a people
> we have a long record of forgiving even those who have been our
> country's most destructive foes.
>
> Yet, to forgive is not to forget the lessons of evil in whatever
> ways evil has operated against us. And certainly the pardon
> granted the former president will not cause us to forget the
> evils of Watergate-type offenses or to forget the lessons we have

learned that a government which deceives its supporters and treats its opponents as enemies must never, never be tolerated.

Whether or not our next president pardons Donald Trump, and whether or not the Department of Justice pursues him, the American people should be told why.

The Justice Department's regional leaders must be copies of an ethical attorney general, at least as to their values. The nature and character of an attorney general for America must be reflected in the people chosen to serve as the United States Attorneys around the country and its territories, especially in the most visible offices. They must radiate the values of the institution in the same way, using their more intimate connection to communities to assure Americans that, in this democracy, Justice is separate from politics and can be trusted. In community meetings, classrooms, and press conferences, they must show their work and their values to the people they serve and protect, while maintaining distance from the political and raising their employees—as I was raised in the Department of Justice—to understand that no case, no embarrassment, no problem is ever worth jeopardizing the reservoir of trust and credibility.

At the FBI, the current director should stay and complete his ten-year-term, created as a symbol of the FBI's distance from the president. Because I know Christopher Wray is a person of integrity, I suspect his silence on the FBI's behalf in the face of Trump's attacks and Barr's defamation was a calculated effort to survive, to avoid giving them an excuse to fire a second director and replace him with a Trumpian loyalist who would be confirmed by the feeble Republican Senate. There was wisdom—and, I suspect, great personal pain—in that approach.

If Wray isn't fired by a spiteful, lame duck Trump, he should, under a new president, feel free to fully radiate the values of his institution, speaking openly and honestly about its shortcomings and its extraordinary strengths, in a way he couldn't when his mission was to survive to protect the institution. The people of the FBI are hurting and need to see and hear from their director, hear his pride in the way they maintained their values during the Trump administration, hear of his plans to improve a remarkable institution and to foster the confidence of the country. As part of saving the Bureau, the director, freed from the shadow of a racist president, can also embrace the essential task of attracting more women and people of color to be special agents and leaders, building an FBI that will be trusted by all Americans. A good start would be a clean break with the FBI's past—and a signal to all of American law enforcement—by removing J. Edgar Hoover's name from the headquarters building and naming it in honor of civil rights icon John Lewis.

It is time for America to move past a fallen and corrupt president and turn to the work of restoration. There is much to do, but the recipe is simple. Tell the American people the truth, about everything. Show them your work, offering transparency about successes and failures. In return, they will give their trust, so the Department of Justice can protect them and serve this great country. Drop by drop, the reservoir will be filled again.

ACKNOWLEDGMENTS

I have much to be thankful for:

The love of my life, for keeping our promise to share a life filled with laughter and joy, and for encouraging me to write this book and helping me think through it.

Our amazing, growing, hilarious, and loving family which, thankfully, constantly finds ways for me to improve.

My partners at Javelin, Keith Urbahn and Matt Latimer, who coached me and made me better from the beginning.

My friends at Flatiron and Macmillan, especially my editor, Zack Wagman, who steered me with grace, humor, and intelligence, all while operating in a pandemic world. I regret only that Marlena Bittner and I won't be able to take the show on the road.

Dave Kelley, Pat Fitzgerald, and Dan Richman, whose counsel and friendship I have treasured for many years, but especially these last four.

And, finally, those who have dedicated their lives to the Department of Justice and built something great. Keep doing good.